Primal Gourmet Diet Cookbook

Unleashing Culinary Excellence with 100+ Satisfying Recipes for a Wholesome and Flavorful Journey

VAKARE RIMKUTE

Copyright © 2024 by Vakare Rimkute

⚠ Disclaimer

The recipes and information presented in this cookbook are intended for general informational purposes only. While Vakare Rimkute has made every effort to ensure the accuracy and completeness of the content, they make no representations or warranties of any kind, express or implied, about the suitability or applicability of the recipes for any purpose

Here is your 28 Days Meal Plan

NB: All recipes are covered in the book

Week One

	Monday	Tuesday	Wednesday
Breakfast	Coconut and Chia Seed Pudding	Gourmet Omelette	Sweet Potato and Bacon Hash
Snacks	Almond Flour Pancakes with Berries	Dark Chocolate Avocado Mousse	Berry and Almond Crumble
Lunch	Grilled Chicken Caesar Salad with Avocado Dressing	Zucchini Noodles with Pesto and Cherry Tomatoes	Smoked Salmon and Avocado Cucumber Bites
Dinner	Beef and Vegetable Bone Broth Soup	Grilled Lemon Garlic Herb Chicken with Cauliflower Mash	Spicy Butternut Squash Soup with Bison and Sweet Potato Sliders

	Thursday	Friday	Saturday
Breakfast	Grilled Chicken Apple Sausage with Eggs	Almond Flour Banana Bread	Berry Blast Smoothie
Snacks	Cucumber and Basil Sparkling Water	Mixed Nuts and Berries	Espresso Chia Seed Pudding
Lunch	Eggplant and Portobello Mushroom Stack	Cabbage and Apple Slaw with Bison	Chicken and Kale Stew with Turmeric
Dinner	Lamb and Lentil Stew	Beef and Vegetable Stir-Fry with Cauliflower Rice	Seared Salmon with Dill Sauce, Roasted Brussels Sprouts

	Sunday
Breakfast	Coconut and Chia Seed Pudding
Snacks	Coconut Flour Banana Bread
Lunch	Grilled Herb-Crusted Rack of Lamb with Asparagus
Dinner	Stuffed Acorn Squash with Quinoa and Cranberries

Week Two

	Monday	Tuesday	Wednesday
Breakfast	Spinach and Mushroom Frittata	Blueberry and Coconut Flour Pancakes	Oatmeal with Nuts and Berries
Snacks	Avocado and Tomato Slices	Carrot Sticks with Guacamole	Apple Slices with Almond Butter
Lunch	Tuna Salad Lettuce Wraps	Greek Salad with Grilled Chicken	Turkey and Avocado Lettuce Wraps
Dinner	Seafood Paella with Cauliflower Rice	Shrimp and Broccoli Stir-Fry with Almond Sauce	Lemon Garlic Roasted Chicken Thighs with Cauliflower Mash

	Thursday	Friday	Saturday
Breakfast	Avocado and Bacon Breakfast Bowl	Smoked Salmon and Dill Scrambled Eggs	Gourmet Green Smoothie
Snacks	Coconut Yogurt Parfait with Berries	Celery Sticks with Almond Butter	Gourmet Energy Bites
Lunch	Caprese Salad with Grilled Chicken	Turkey and Vegetable Skewers with Chimichurri Sauce	Roasted Vegetable Salad with Balsamic Glaze
Dinner	Beef and Broccoli Stir-Fry with Sesame Seeds	Creamy Mushroom and Spinach Stuffed Chicken Breast	Grilled Swordfish with Mango Salsa

	Sunday
Breakfast	Chia Seed and Berry Smoothie Bowl
Snacks	Mixed Berries with Coconut Whipped Cream
Lunch	Shrimp and Avocado Salad
Dinner	Moroccan Spiced Lamb Chops with Cauliflower Couscous

Week Three

	Monday	Tuesday	Wednesday
Breakfast	Burrito with Lettuce Wrap	Banana Almond Butter Smoothie	Blueberry Coconut Flour Muffins
Snacks	Gourmet Trail Mix	Cucumber Slices with Hummus	Guacamole with Jicama Chips
Lunch	Chicken and Vegetable Kebabs with Tzatziki Sauce	Thai-Inspired Beef Salad with Mint and Cilantro	Spinach and Strawberry Salad with Grilled Chicken
Dinner	Grilled Halibut with Lemon Herb Sauce, Roasted Brussels Sprouts	Baked Cod with Tomato and Olive Relish	Pork Tenderloin with Apple Cider Glaze, Roasted Sweet Potatoes

	Thursday	Friday	Saturday
Breakfast	Breakfast Bowl with Mixed Berries	Breakfast Sausage Patties	Mango Coconut Chia Pudding
Snacks	Greek Yogurt with Walnuts and Honey	Veggie Chips with Guacamole	Almond and Coconut Energy Balls
Lunch	Tuna and Avocado Salad	Quinoa and Grilled Vegetable Bowl	Waldorf Chicken Salad
Dinner	Herb-Crusted Turkey Breast with Cranberry Relish, Sautéed Green Beans	Lemon Herb Grilled Shrimp Skewers, Cauliflower Rice	Bison and Sweet Potato Chili

	Sunday
Breakfast	Frittata with Spinach and Feta
Snacks	Raspberry Coconut Chia Popsicles
Lunch	Greek Chicken Souvlaki with Tzatziki Sauce
Dinner	Beef and Vegetable Stir-Fry with Broccoli and Cashews

Week Four

	Monday	Tuesday	Wednesday
Breakfast	Almond Flour Waffles with Fresh Berries	Almond Flour Crepes with Mixed Berries	Coconut Flour Pancakes with Almond Butter
Snacks	Kale Chips	Protein Balls	Mixed Nuts and Dried Fruits
Lunch	Caprese Stuffed Avocado	Turkey and Avocado BLT Lettuce Wraps	Shrimp and Mango Salad
Dinner	Grilled Salmon with Cilantro Lime Marinade, Asparagus	Spaghetti Squash with Bolognese Sauce	Herb-Roasted Chicken Thighs with Roasted Vegetables

	Thursday	Friday	Saturday
Breakfast	Blueberry and Almond Butter Smoothie	Banana Bread with Walnuts	Avocado and Egg Breakfast Muffins
Snacks	Deviled Eggs	Greek Yogurt Parfait with Granola	Zucchini Fritters
Lunch	Chicken Caesar Salad Wrap with Lettuce	Mediterranean Quinoa Bowl with Grilled Vegetables	Tuna Poke Bowl with Cauliflower Rice
Dinner	Chicken Caesar Salad Wrap with Lettuce	Lemon Dill Baked Cod, Steamed Broccoli	Pork Carnitas Lettuce Wraps with Pico de Gallo

	Sunday
Breakfast	Almond Flour Crepes with Mixed Berries
Snacks	Dark Chocolate Covered Strawberries
Lunch	Egg Salad Lettuce Wraps
Dinner	Sesame Ginger Glazed Salmon, Stir-Fried Bok Choy

Table of Contents

Introduction to Primal Cooking

Breakfasts

Lunch

Caprese Stuffed Avocado

Greek Chicken Souvlaki with Tzatziki Sauce

Quinoa and Grilled Vegetable Bowl

Shrimp and Mango Salad

Spinach and Strawberry Salad with Grilled Chicken

Thai-Inspired Beef Salad with Mint and Cilantro

Greek Salad with Grilled Chicken

Shrimp and Avocado Salad

Chicken and Vegetable Kebabs with Tzatziki Sauce

Roasted Vegetable Salad with Balsamic Glaze

Caprese Salad with Grilled Chicken

Turkey and Vegetable Skewers with Chimichurri Sauce

Dinner

Beef and Vegetable Bone Broth Soup

Grilled Lemon Garlic Herb Chicken with Cauliflower Mash

Spicy Butternut Squash Soup

Bison and Sweet Potato Sliders

Seared Salmon with Dill Sauce

Roasted Brussels Sprouts

Lemon Herb Grilled Shrimp Skewers

Sesame Ginger Glazed Salmon

Beef and Vegetable Kebabs with Cilantro Lime

Grilled Lamb Chops with Mint Pesto

Pork Carnitas Lettuce Wraps with Pico de Gallo

Lemon Dill Baked Cod

Grilled Steak with Chimichurri Sauce

Spaghetti Squash with Bolognese Sauce

Herb-Roasted Chicken Thighs with Roasted Vegetables

Grilled Salmon with Cilantro Lime Marinade

Beef and Vegetable Stir-Fry with Broccoli and Cashews

Pork Tenderloin with Apple Cider Glaze

Baked Cod with Tomato and Olive Relish

Lamb and Lentil Stew

Stuffed Acorn Squash with Quinoa and Cranberries

Seafood Paella with Cauliflower Rice

Shrimp and Broccoli Stir-Fry with Almond Sauce

Herb-crusted Turkey Breast with Cranberry Relish Sautéed Green Beans

Moroccan Spiced Lamb Chops with Cauliflower Couscous

Grilled Halibut with Lemon Herb Sauce

Lemon Garlic Roasted Chicken Thighs

Creamy Mushroom and Spinach Stuffed Chicken Breast

Grilled Swordfish with Mango Salsa

Snacks

Almond Flour Pancakes with Berries

Dark Chocolate Avocado Mousse

Berry and Almond Crumble

Espresso Chia Seed Pudding

Cucumber and Basil Sparkling Water

Coconut Flour Banana Bread

Mixed Nuts and Berries

Deviled Eggs

Greek Yogurt Parfait with Granola

Dark Chocolate Covered Strawberries

Zucchini Fritters

Seaweed Snacks

Avocado and Tomato Slices

Carrot Sticks with Guacamole

Coconut Yogurt with Berries

Apple Slices with Almond Butter

Kale Chips

Protein Balls

Almond and Coconut Energy Balls

Celery Sticks with Almond Butter

Mixed Nuts and Dried Fruits

Gourmet Energy Bites

Mixed Berries with Coconut Whipped Cream

Gourmet Trail Mix

Veggie Chips with Guacamole

Raspberry Coconut Chia Popsicles

Cucumber Slices with Hummus

Guacamole with Jicama Chips

Greek Yogurt with Walnuts and Honey

Conclusion

Introduction

Welcome to *"Primal Gourmet Diet Cookbook,"* a culinary journey that transcends the boundaries of ordinary cooking and invites you to embrace a lifestyle that prioritizes nourishment, flavour, and overall well-being. In the following pages, we embark on a flavorful exploration of primal cooking, celebrating the goodness of whole, unprocessed foods and the art of crafting delicious, nutrient-dense meals.

At the heart of this cookbook lies the Primal Gourmet philosophy, a commitment to harnessing the inherent goodness of natural, high-quality ingredients. Drawing inspiration from the primal diet, we focus on nourishing the body with lean proteins, vibrant vegetables, healthy fats, and a myriad of whole foods that have sustained humanity for generations. This philosophy extends beyond a simple collection of recipes; it's a holistic approach to wellness, emphasizing the profound connection between the food we consume and our overall health.

13

*"**Primal Gourmet Diet Cookbook**"* isn't just a compilation of recipes; it's a guide to a lifestyle that brings forth an array of benefits. From supporting weight management and regulating blood sugar to fostering gut health and reducing inflammation, the recipes presented here are designed to enhance your culinary experience and overall vitality. Embrace the potential for increased energy, improved mental clarity, and a sense of well-being that comes with embracing a primal approach to cooking and eating.

To kickstart your primal culinary adventure, we've included a 30-day meal plan featuring a diverse array of breakfasts, lunches, dinners, and snacks. This carefully curated plan ensures that you experience the variety and deliciousness that a primal lifestyle can offer, all while providing the nutrients your body craves.

*"**Primal Gourmet Diet Cookbook**"* is more than just a collection of recipes; it's an invitation to transform the way you approach food, savouring the joy of cooking and nourishing your body with every bite. Join us to embrace the primal gourmet lifestyle — a celebration of food, flavour, and well-being that transcends the ordinary. Let's embark on a culinary adventure together, one delicious and nutritious meal at a time.

Let get started

Sweet Potato and Bacon Hash

Directions

- Peel and dice the sweet potatoes into small, bite-sized cubes.
- Heat a large skillet over medium heat.
- Add the chopped bacon to the skillet and cook until it becomes crispy.
- Once the bacon is crispy, remove it from the skillet and set it aside.
- In the same skillet, using the bacon grease, add the diced sweet potatoes.
- Cook the sweet potatoes until they are golden brown and cooked through. This usually takes about 10-15 minutes.
- Add the diced onion, minced garlic, and bell pepper to the skillet with the sweet potatoes.
- Sauté the mixture until the vegetables are tender.
- Season the hash with salt and pepper to taste.
- Once the vegetables are cooked, add the crispy bacon back into the skillet.
- Toss everything together until well combined and heated through.
- Garnish with fresh chopped parsley before serving.

Ingredients

- 2 medium sweet potatoes, peeled and diced
- 6 slices of bacon, chopped
- 1 onion, diced
- 2 cloves garlic, minced
- 1 bell pepper, diced
- Salt and pepper, to taste
- Fresh parsley, chopped (for garnish)

Coconut and Chia Seed Pudding

Directions

- In a bowl, combine the chia seeds, coconut milk, honey or maple syrup, vanilla extract, and a pinch of salt. Stir the mixture well to ensure the chia seeds are evenly distributed.
- Cover the bowl and refrigerate the mixture for at least 4 hours or preferably overnight. This allows the chia seeds to absorb the liquid and create a pudding-like consistency.
- During the first hour of refrigeration, stir the mixture every 15-20 minutes to prevent clumping of chia seeds. This ensures a smoother pudding texture.
- After the initial soaking, taste the pudding and adjust the sweetness according to your preference by adding more honey or maple syrup if needed. Stir well.
- Once the chia seeds have absorbed the liquid and the pudding has thickened, it's ready to be served. Spoon the pudding into serving bowls or jars.
- Add a generous topping of fresh berries or sliced fruits on top of the pudding. The combination of coconut and fruit enhances the flavour.
- If desired, garnish the pudding with shredded coconut for added texture and a hint of coconut flavour.
- Serve the Coconut and Chia Seed Pudding chilled. It makes a delicious and nutritious breakfast, snack, or dessert.

Ingredients

- 1/4 cup chia seeds
- 1 cup coconut milk (full-fat for creamier consistency)
- 1-2 tablespoons honey or maple syrup (adjust to taste)
- 1/2 teaspoon vanilla extract
- A pinch of salt
- Fresh berries or sliced fruits for topping
- Shredded coconut for garnish (optional)

16

Berry Blast Smoothie

Directions

- Wash and clean the berries.
- Peel and freeze half of a banana.
- In a blender, add the mixed berries and frozen banana.
- Spoon in the Greek yoghurt.
- Pour the almond milk into the blender.
- Sprinkle the chia seeds into the mix.
- If you prefer a sweeter smoothie, add honey or maple syrup to taste.
-
- Blend all the ingredients until you achieve a smooth and creamy consistency. If the smoothie is too thick, you can add more almond milk.
- If desired, add ice cubes and blend again until the smoothie reaches your preferred thickness.
- Pour the Berry Blast Smoothie into a glass, and enjoy the refreshing and nutritious blend of berries.

Ingredients

- 1 cup mixed berries (strawberries, blueberries, raspberries)
- 1/2 banana, frozen
- 1/2 cup plain Greek yogurt
- 1/2 cup almond milk (or any preferred milk)
- 1 tablespoon chia seeds
- 1 tablespoon honey or maple syrup (optional, depending on sweetness preference)
- Ice cubes (optional)

Grilled Chicken Apple Sausage with Eggs

Directions

- Preheat an outdoor grill or grill pan over medium-high heat.
- Place the chicken apple sausages on the preheated grill.
- Grill for 8-10 minutes, turning occasionally, until they are fully cooked and have nice grill marks on all sides.
- While the sausages are grilling, heat olive oil in a skillet over medium heat.
- Add the thinly sliced apple to the skillet and sprinkle with ground cinnamon.
- Sauté the apples for 4-5 minutes until they are tender but still have a slight crunch. Remove from heat and set aside.
- In the same skillet, crack the eggs and cook them to your liking (scrambled, fried, or poached).
- Season the eggs with salt and pepper.
- Place the grilled chicken apple sausages on a serving plate.
- Arrange the sautéed cinnamon apples around the sausages.
- Top the sausages and apples with the cooked eggs.
- Garnish the dish with chopped fresh parsley if desired.
- Serve immediately while everything is hot.

Ingredients

- 4 chicken apple sausages
- 4 large eggs
- 1 tablespoon olive oil
- 1 medium apple, cored and thinly sliced
- 1/2 teaspoon ground cinnamon
- Salt and pepper, to taste
- Fresh parsley, chopped (for garnish, optional)

18

Golden Milk Chia Pudding

Directions

- In a bowl, combine the chia seeds, ground turmeric, ground cinnamon, ground ginger, and ground cardamom. Mix well to ensure even distribution.
- Pour the almond milk into the bowl with the dry ingredients.
- Add the maple syrup (or honey), vanilla extract, and a pinch of black pepper.
- Stir the mixture thoroughly to combine all the ingredients.
- Let the mixture sit for a few minutes and then stir again to prevent clumping.
- Cover the bowl and refrigerate the mixture for at least 4 hours or preferably overnight. This allows the chia seeds to absorb the liquid and create a pudding-like consistency.
- After the initial refrigeration, check the pudding. If it's too thick, you can add a bit more almond milk and stir to reach your desired consistency.
- Spoon the golden milk chia pudding into serving bowls or jars.
- Optionally, top with sliced almonds, shredded coconut, and fresh berries for added texture and flavour.
- Serve chilled and enjoy your Golden Milk Chia Pudding as a delightful and nutritious breakfast, snack, or dessert.

Ingredients

- 1/4 cup chia seeds
- 1 cup unsweetened almond milk (or any milk of your choice)
- 1 teaspoon ground turmeric
- 1/2 teaspoon ground cinnamon
- 1/4 teaspoon ground ginger
- 1/4 teaspoon ground cardamom
- 1-2 tablespoons maple syrup or honey (adjust to taste)
- 1/2 teaspoon vanilla extract
- A pinch of black pepper (enhances turmeric absorption)
- Optional toppings: sliced almonds, shredded coconut, and fresh berries

19

Almond Flour Banana Bread

Directions

- Preheat your oven to 350°F (175°C).
- Grease a standard-sized loaf pan or line it with parchment paper.
- In a large mixing bowl, mash the ripe bananas with a fork or potato masher until smooth.
- Add the eggs, melted coconut oil, and vanilla extract to the mashed bananas. Mix well until the ingredients are combined.
- In a separate bowl, whisk together the almond flour, baking soda, baking powder, cinnamon, and salt.
- Gradually add the dry ingredients to the wet ingredients, stirring until just combined. Be careful not to overmix.
- If you're using nuts, fold them into the batter until evenly distributed.
- Pour the batter into the prepared loaf pan, spreading it out evenly.
- Bake in the preheated oven for 45-55 minutes or until a toothpick inserted into the centre comes out clean.
- Allow the banana bread to cool in the pan for about 10 minutes, then transfer it to a wire rack to cool completely.
- Once cooled, slice the banana bread into pieces and serve. Enjoy!

Ingredients

- 3 ripe bananas, mashed
- 3 large eggs
- 1/4 cup coconut oil, melted
- 1 teaspoon vanilla extract
- 2 cups almond flour
- 1 teaspoon baking soda
- 1/2 teaspoon baking powder
- 1/2 teaspoon cinnamon
- 1/4 teaspoon salt
- Optional: 1/2 cup chopped nuts (such as walnuts or pecans)

20

Spinach and Mushroom Frittata

Directions

- Preheat your oven to 375°F (190°C).
- In a skillet, heat 1 tablespoon of olive oil over medium heat. Add the chopped onion and cook until softened about 2-3 minutes. Add the sliced mushrooms and minced garlic, and sauté until the mushrooms are browned and the excess moisture has evaporated about 5-7 minutes. Add the chopped spinach and cook for an additional 2 minutes until wilted. Season with salt and pepper.
- In a mixing bowl, whisk together the eggs and milk until well combined. Season with salt and pepper.
- Pour the whisked eggs over the sautéed vegetables in the skillet. Allow the eggs to settle around the vegetables. If using feta cheese, sprinkle it evenly over the eggs.
- Cook the frittata on the stovetop over medium heat for about 3-4 minutes, allowing the edges to set.
- Transfer the skillet to the preheated oven and bake for 12-15 minutes or until the frittata is set in the centre and the top is lightly golden brown.
- If you want a golden top, you can briefly broil the frittata for 1-2 minutes until it's golden and slightly puffed.
- Garnish and Serve: Remove the frittata from the oven, garnish with fresh herbs, and let it cool for a few minutes. Slice it into wedges and serve warm.

Ingredients

- 8 large eggs
- 1/2 cup milk (or a dairy-free alternative)
- 1 cup fresh spinach, chopped
- 1 cup mushrooms, sliced
- 1/2 onion, finely chopped
- 1 garlic clove, minced
- 1/2 cup feta cheese, crumbled (optional)
- Salt and pepper, to taste
- 2 tablespoons olive oil
- Fresh herbs for garnish (e.g., parsley or chives)

21

Blueberry and Coconut Flour Pancakes

Directions

- In a large mixing bowl, whisk together the coconut flour, baking powder, and a pinch of salt.
- In a separate bowl, beat the eggs. Add the coconut milk, melted coconut oil, honey or maple syrup (if using), and vanilla extract. Mix well.
- Pour the wet ingredients into the bowl with the dry ingredients and stir until well combined. Let the batter sit for a few minutes to allow the coconut flour to absorb the liquid.
- Gently fold in the fresh blueberries.
- Heat a griddle or non-stick skillet over medium heat. If needed, lightly grease the surface with coconut oil.
- Spoon the pancake batter onto the griddle, using about 1/4 cup of batter for each pancake. Use the back of the spoon to spread the batter into a round shape.
- Cook the pancakes until small bubbles form on the surface, then carefully flip them with a spatula. Cook for an additional 1-2 minutes on the other side, or until golden brown.
- Repeat the process with the remaining batter, adjusting the heat if necessary.
- Serve the pancakes warm, topped with additional blueberries, a drizzle of honey or maple syrup, and any other desired toppings.

Ingredients

- 1/2 cup coconut flour
- 1 teaspoon baking powder
- Pinch of salt
- 4 large eggs
- 1 cup coconut milk (or any other milk of your choice)
- 2 tablespoons melted coconut oil
- 1 tablespoon honey or maple syrup (optional, for sweetness)
- 1 teaspoon vanilla extract
- 1 cup fresh blueberries (or frozen, thawed)
-

Oatmeal with Nuts and Berries

Directions

- In a saucepan, combine the old-fashioned oats and almond milk. Add a pinch of salt and bring the mixture to a gentle boil over medium heat.
- Once the mixture starts boiling, reduce the heat to low and let it simmer. Stir occasionally to prevent the oats from sticking to the bottom of the pan.
- After a few minutes, add chia seeds to the simmering oats. Stir well to combine. The chia seeds will absorb liquid and add thickness to the oatmeal.
- Continue cooking and stirring until the oatmeal reaches your desired consistency. If it becomes too thick, you can add a bit more almond milk.
- Stir in the vanilla extract to enhance the flavour of the oatmeal.
- If desired, sweeten the oatmeal with pure maple syrup or honey. Adjust the sweetness to your liking.
- Once the oatmeal is creamy and cooked to your preference, remove the saucepan from the heat.
- Serve the oatmeal in bowls, and top each serving with a generous sprinkle of chopped mixed nuts and fresh berries.
- Feel free to add extra toppings such as sliced banana, coconut flakes, or a dollop of yoghurt for added flavour and texture.
- Grab a spoon and enjoy your delicious Primal Oatmeal with Nuts and Berries!

Ingredients

- 1 cup old-fashioned oats (choose gluten-free oats if necessary)
- 2 cups almond milk (or any other non-dairy milk of your choice)
- 1 tablespoon chia seeds
- 1/4 cup chopped mixed nuts (e.g., almonds, walnuts, pecans)
- 1/4 cup fresh berries (e.g., blueberries, raspberries, strawberries)
- 1 tablespoon pure maple syrup or honey (optional, for sweetness)
- Pinch of salt
- 1/2 teaspoon vanilla extract
- Additional toppings (optional): sliced banana, coconut flakes, or a dollop of yoghurt

23

Gourmet Omelette

Directions

- Chop all vegetables and set aside.
- If you're adding optional toppings, prepare them now.
- Crack the eggs into a bowl and whisk them until well combined.
- Season with a pinch of salt and pepper.
- Heat 1 tablespoon of olive oil or ghee in a non-stick skillet over medium heat.
- Add diced red and green bell peppers, red onion, mushrooms, and baby spinach.
- Sauté the vegetables until they are softened, about 3-4 minutes.
- Push the sautéed vegetables to one side of the skillet.
- Add the remaining 1 tablespoon of oil or ghee to the empty side.
- Pour the whisked eggs into the empty side of the skillet.
- Use a spatula to gently swirl the eggs, allowing them to coat the bottom of the skillet and mix with the sautéed vegetables.
- Let the eggs cook undisturbed for a minute, then gently lift the edges with the spatula to let any uncooked egg flow underneath.
- Once the edges are set but the center is still slightly runny, fold one side of the omelette over the vegetables.
- Cook for an additional 1-2 minutes until the eggs are fully set but still moist.
- Slide the omelette onto a plate, folding it over itself if necessary.
- Garnish with optional toppings like avocado slices, cherry tomatoes, or fresh herbs.
- Serve your Primal Gourmet Omelette hot and enjoy a delicious, nutrient-packed breakfast!

Ingredients

- 3 large eggs, preferably free-range or organic
- 2 tablespoons olive oil or ghee
- 1/4 cup diced red bell pepper
- 1/4 cup diced green bell pepper
- 1/4 cup diced red onion
- 1/4 cup sliced mushrooms
- 1/4 cup baby spinach, chopped
- Salt and pepper, to taste
- Optional toppings: avocado slices, cherry tomatoes, fresh herbs (e.g., parsley or chives)

Chorizo and Green Bean Casserole

Directions

- Preheat your oven to 375°F (190°C).
- Bring a large pot of salted water to a boil. Add the green beans and blanch for 3-4 minutes until they are bright green but still crisp. Drain and immediately transfer to a bowl of ice water to stop the cooking process. Drain again and set aside.
- In a large skillet over medium heat, cook the crumbled chorizo until browned and cooked through. Remove excess fat if necessary.
- In the same skillet, add a bit of olive oil if needed. Add chopped onion and sauté until softened, about 3-4 minutes. Add minced garlic and cook for an additional 1-2 minutes until fragrant.
- Stir in sliced mushrooms and halved cherry tomatoes. Cook for 5-6 minutes until the mushrooms are tender and the tomatoes start to release their juices.
- Add the cooked chorizo back to the skillet with the vegetables. Mix well to combine.
- In a separate saucepan, combine chicken or vegetable broth, heavy cream, and smoked paprika. Bring to a simmer over medium heat. Season with salt and pepper to taste.
- In a large baking dish, combine the blanched green beans with the chorizo and vegetable mixture. Pour the sauce over the top and gently toss to coat everything evenly.
- Sprinkle shredded cheddar cheese over the casserole.
- Bake in the preheated oven for 20-25 minutes or until the casserole is bubbly, and the cheese is melted and golden brown.
- Remove from the oven, garnish with fresh parsley if desired, and let it rest for a few minutes before serving.
- Scoop out generous servings of this delicious Chorizo and Green Bean Casserole and enjoy!

Ingredients

- 1 lb fresh green beans, trimmed and halved
- 1 lb chorizo sausage, casing removed and crumbled
- 1 large onion, finely chopped
- 3 cloves garlic, minced
- 1 cup mushrooms, sliced
- 1 cup cherry tomatoes, halved
- 1 cup chicken or vegetable broth
- 1 cup heavy cream
- 1 cup shredded cheddar cheese
- 1 teaspoon smoked paprika
- Salt and pepper to taste
- Olive oil for cooking
- Fresh parsley for garnish (optional)

Avocado and Bacon Breakfast Bowl

Directions

- Preheat your oven to 375°F (190°C).
- Place bacon slices on a baking sheet lined with parchment paper.
- Bake in the preheated oven for 15-20 minutes or until the bacon is crispy.
- Remove from the oven and let it cool. Once cooled, crumble the bacon into bits.
- Cut the avocados in half and remove the pits.
- Scoop out a small portion of the flesh from each avocado half to create a well for the eggs.
- Heat olive oil in a non-stick skillet over medium heat.
- Place the hollowed-out avocados in the skillet to stabilize them.
- Crack one egg into each avocado half, being careful not to overflow.
- Season each egg with salt and pepper to taste.
- Cover the skillet with a lid and cook for 8-10 minutes or until the egg whites are set, but the yolks are still runny. Adjust the cooking time for your desired egg consistency.
- Carefully transfer the avocado halves with the cooked eggs onto serving plates.
- Sprinkle crumbled bacon over the eggs in each avocado half.
- Garnish with cherry tomatoes, chopped chives, or a drizzle of hot sauce for extra flavour and freshness.
- Serve the Avocado and Bacon Breakfast Bowls immediately while the eggs are still warm.

Ingredients

- 2 ripe avocados
- 6 slices of nitrate-free bacon
- 4 large eggs
- 1 tablespoon olive oil
- Salt and pepper to taste
- Optional toppings: cherry tomatoes, chopped chives, hot sauce

26

Smoked Salmon and Dill Scrambled Eggs

Directions

- Crack the eggs into a bowl, add milk or cream, and whisk together until well combined.
- Season the egg mixture with salt and pepper according to your taste.
- Thinly slice the smoked salmon and chop the fresh dill.
- In a non-stick skillet, melt the butter over medium heat.
- Pour the whisked egg mixture into the skillet, ensuring an even spread.
- Allow the eggs to sit for a moment until the edges begin to set.
- With a spatula, gently push the eggs from the edges toward the centre, allowing the uncooked eggs to flow to the edges.
- When the eggs are mostly set but still slightly runny, add the thinly sliced smoked salmon to the skillet.
- Continue to scramble the eggs, incorporating the smoked salmon evenly. Cook until the eggs are fully set but still moist.
- Sprinkle chopped fresh dill over the scrambled eggs and mix it in just before the eggs finish cooking. The dill adds a burst of freshness and complements the smoked salmon.
- Once the eggs are cooked to your liking, remove the skillet from heat.
- Plate the scrambled eggs and smoked salmon, garnishing with additional dill if desired.
- Serve with lemon wedges on the side for a citrusy touch (optional).

Ingredients

- 4 large eggs
- 1/4 cup milk or cream
- Salt and pepper to taste
- 2 tablespoons unsalted butter
- 100g smoked salmon, thinly sliced
- 1 tablespoon fresh dill, chopped
- Lemon wedges for serving (optional)

Blueberry and Almond Butter Smoothie

Directions

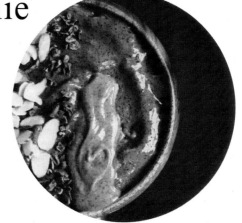

- If you haven't done so already, freeze the blueberries in advance.
- Peel and slice the banana.
- In a blender, add the frozen blueberries, sliced banana, almond butter, almond milk, Greek yoghurt, and chia seeds (if using).
- If you prefer a colder and thicker smoothie, you can also add a handful of ice cubes.
- Blend the ingredients on high speed until the mixture is smooth and creamy. This usually takes about 1-2 minutes.
- If the smoothie is too thick, you can add more almond milk, a little at a time, until you reach your desired consistency.
- Taste the smoothie and adjust the sweetness if needed. You can add a touch of honey or maple syrup if you prefer it sweeter.
- Pour the smoothie into a glass and enjoy immediately.

Ingredients

- 1 cup frozen blueberries
- 1 banana, peeled and sliced
- 1 tablespoon almond butter
- 1 cup almond milk (or any milk of your choice)
- 1/2 cup Greek yogurt
- 1 tablespoon chia seeds (optional)
- Ice cubes (optional)

Optional Additions:

- A handful of spinach or kale for added greens and nutrients.
- A scoop of protein powder for an extra protein boost.
- A drizzle of honey or a sprinkle of cinnamon for additional flavor.

Gourmet Green Smoothie

Directions

- Wash the kale and spinach thoroughly. Remove the stems from the kale and tear the leaves into smaller pieces.
- Peel and slice the cucumber.
- Peel and pit the avocado.
- Core and chop the green apple.
- In a blender, combine the torn kale leaves, spinach, sliced cucumber, avocado, chopped green apple, chia seeds, and flaxseeds.
- Pour in the coconut water or almond milk.
- Squeeze the juice of half a lemon into the blender. Adjust the amount based on your taste preferences.
- Blend the ingredients on high speed until you achieve a smooth and creamy consistency. If the smoothie is too thick, you can add more liquid.
- If desired, add ice cubes to the blender and blend again until the smoothie reaches your preferred consistency.
- Pour the Gourmet Green Smoothie into a glass and garnish with a slice of cucumber or a sprinkle of chia seeds, if desired.
- Customize your smoothie by adding a scoop of protein powder, a handful of mint leaves, or a teaspoon of honey for added sweetness.
- Experiment with different greens such as arugula or Swiss chard.
- Adjust the sweetness by adding more apples or incorporating other fruits like pineapple or kiwi.

Ingredients

- 1 cup kale, stems removed and leaves torn
- 1/2 cup spinach leaves
- 1/2 cucumber, peeled and sliced
- 1/2 avocado, peeled and pitted
- 1/2 green apple, cored and chopped
- 1/2 lemon, juiced
- 1 tablespoon chia seeds
- 1 tablespoon flaxseeds
- 1 cup coconut water or almond milk
- Ice cubes (optional)

29

Breakfast Burrito with Lettuce Wrap

Directions

- Wash and pat dry the iceberg lettuce leaves.
- Lay the leaves flat on a clean surface, ensuring they are dry.
- In a medium-sized skillet, heat the ghee or coconut oil over medium heat.
- Add the diced bell peppers and red onion to the skillet. Sauté until softened, about 3-4 minutes.
- Crack the eggs into a bowl and whisk them together.
- Pour the whisked eggs into the skillet with the sautéed vegetables.
- Stir continuously until the eggs are scrambled and fully cooked.
- Season the scrambled eggs with salt and pepper to taste.
- Stir in the diced tomatoes and chopped cilantro, cooking for an additional 1-2 minutes.
- Spoon a portion of the scrambled egg mixture onto each lettuce leaf.
- Add optional toppings such as salsa, sliced avocado, or hot sauce.
- Carefully fold the sides of the lettuce leaves over the filling.
- Secure the wraps with toothpicks if needed.
- Arrange the breakfast burrito lettuce wraps on a serving platter.
- Serve immediately and enjoy your Primal Gourmet Breakfast Burrito!

Ingredients

- 4 large iceberg lettuce leaves (for wraps)
- 4 large eggs
- 1 tablespoon ghee or coconut oil
- 1/2 cup diced bell peppers (mix of colors)
- 1/2 cup diced red onion
- 1/2 cup diced tomatoes
- 1/4 cup chopped fresh cilantro
- Salt and pepper to taste
- Optional toppings: salsa, sliced avocado, hot sauce

Chi Seed and Berry Smoothie Bowl

Directions

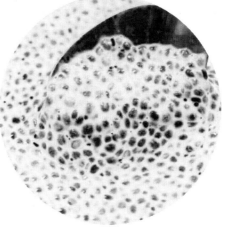

- In a small bowl, mix 1/4 cup of almond milk with the chia seeds. Stir well and let it sit for at least 15-20 minutes or until it forms a gel-like consistency. You can also prepare this the night before and leave it in the refrigerator.
- In a blender, combine the mixed berries, frozen banana, Greek yoghurt, remaining almond milk, and honey or maple syrup if using.
- Blend until smooth and creamy. If the mixture is too thick, you can add more almond milk as needed.
- Pour the smoothie into a bowl.
- Arrange sliced strawberries, blueberries, chia seeds, granola, shredded coconut, and sliced almonds on top of the smoothie.
- Take the prepared chia seed pudding and drizzle it over the smoothie bowl.
- Serve the Chia Seed and Berry Smoothie Bowl immediately, and enjoy with a spoon!

Ingredients

For the Smoothie:

- 1 cup mixed berries (strawberries, blueberries, raspberries)
- 1 ripe banana, frozen
- 1/2 cup Greek yogurt
- 1 tablespoon chia seeds
- 1/2 cup almond milk (or any milk of your choice)
- 1 teaspoon honey or maple syrup (optional, for sweetness)
- Ice cubes (optional)

For Toppings:

- Sliced strawberries
- Blueberries
- Chia seeds
- Granola
- Shredded coconut
- Sliced almonds

Banana Almond Butter Smoothie

Directions

- Peel and slice the ripe banana.
- In a blender, add the sliced banana, almond milk, almond butter, ground cinnamon, and vanilla extract.
- If you want to add extra protein to your smoothie, include a scoop of your favourite protein powder at this point.
- Blend the ingredients on high speed until the mixture is smooth and creamy. If you prefer a thicker consistency, you can add more ice cubes.
- Taste the smoothie and adjust the sweetness or thickness by adding more almond milk or ice cubes if necessary.
- Pour the Banana Almond Butter Smoothie into a glass.
- Garnish with a sprinkle of cinnamon or a few sliced almonds for added texture.
- Sip and enjoy your delicious and nutritious Banana Almond Butter Smoothie!

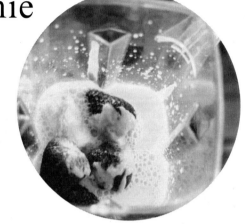

Ingredients

- 1 ripe banana, peeled and sliced
- 1 cup almond milk (unsweetened)
- 1 tablespoon almond butter
- 1/2 teaspoon ground cinnamon
- 1/2 teaspoon vanilla extract
- 1 cup ice cubes (optional for a colder smoothie)
- Optional: 1 scoop of your favorite protein powder for added protein
-

Blueberry Coconut Flour Muffins

Directions

- Preheat your oven to 350°F (175°C). Line a muffin tin with paper liners or grease the muffin cups.
- In a large mixing bowl, whisk together the coconut flour, almond flour, coconut sugar, baking powder, baking soda, and salt. Ensure that there are no lumps.
- In another bowl, beat the eggs. Add in the coconut milk, melted coconut oil, and vanilla extract. Mix well until everything is well combined.
- Pour the wet ingredients into the bowl with the dry ingredients. Mix until just combined. Be careful not to overmix, as coconut flour can absorb a lot of moisture.
- Gently fold the blueberries into the batter until evenly distributed.
- Using a spoon or an ice cream scoop, fill each muffin cup about 3/4 full with the batter.
- Bake in the preheated oven for 20-25 minutes or until a toothpick inserted into the centre of a muffin comes out clean.
- Allow the muffins to cool in the tin for a few minutes, then transfer them to a wire rack to cool completely.
- Once cooled, these Blueberry Coconut Flour Muffins are ready to be enjoyed! Serve them as a delicious breakfast or snack.

Ingredients

- 1 cup coconut flour
- 1/2 cup almond flour
- 1/2 cup coconut sugar or sweetener of choice
- 1 teaspoon baking powder
- 1/2 teaspoon baking soda
- 1/4 teaspoon salt
- 4 large eggs
- 1 cup coconut milk (or any milk of your choice)
- 1/4 cup melted coconut oil
- 1 teaspoon vanilla extract
- 1 cup fresh or frozen blueberries

Breakfast Bowl with Mixed Berries

Directions

- Wash the mixed berries thoroughly and pat them dry with a paper towel.
- If using strawberries, hull and slice them. Leave smaller berries whole.
- In a bowl, start with a base of Greek yoghurt or coconut yoghurt.
- Arrange the mixed berries on top of the yoghurt. Be creative with the arrangement for an appealing presentation.
- Warm the almond butter slightly to make it easier to drizzle. Use a spoon to drizzle the almond butter over the berries.
- Sprinkle chia seeds and shredded coconut evenly over the berries and almond butter.
- Sprinkle chopped nuts over the bowl for added crunch and a boost of healthy fats.
- If you prefer a sweeter breakfast, drizzle honey or maple syrup over the top. Adjust the sweetness according to your taste.
- For a refreshing touch, garnish the bowl with fresh mint leaves.
- Your Primal Gourmet Breakfast Bowl with Mixed Berries is ready to be enjoyed! Use a spoon to mix the ingredients before digging in.

Ingredients

- 1 cup mixed berries (strawberries, blueberries, raspberries, blackberries)
- 1/2 cup Greek yogurt or coconut yogurt for a dairy-free option
- 2 tablespoons almond butter
- 1 tablespoon chia seeds
- 1 tablespoon shredded coconut
- 1 tablespoon chopped nuts (walnuts, almonds, or pecans)
- 1 teaspoon honey or maple syrup (optional, for sweetness)
- Fresh mint leaves for garnish (optional)

34

Breakfast Sausage Patties

Directions

- In a small bowl, mix together the salt, black pepper, dried sage, dried thyme, dried rosemary, garlic powder, onion powder, paprika, and cayenne pepper. Ensure the spices are well combined.
- Place the ground pork in a large mixing bowl. Sprinkle the spice mixture over the ground pork.
- Using your hands or a spoon, mix the ground pork and spices thoroughly. Make sure the spices are evenly distributed throughout the meat.
- Divide the seasoned pork mixture into equal portions and shape them into patties. You can adjust the size based on your preference.
  - **Stovetop:** Heat a skillet or frying pan over medium heat. Add a little cooking fat of your choice (e.g., coconut oil, ghee). Cook the sausage patties for about 3-4 minutes per side or until fully cooked and browned on the outside.
  - **Oven:** Preheat the oven to 375°F (190°C). Place the patties on a baking sheet lined with parchment paper. Bake for approximately 15-20 minutes, flipping halfway through, until cooked through.
  - Once the sausage patties are cooked through and have a nice brown crust, remove them from the heat. Allow them to rest for a minute before serving.

Ingredients

- 1 pound ground pork (preferably pasture-raised)
- 1 teaspoon salt
- 1/2 teaspoon black pepper
- 1/2 teaspoon dried sage
- 1/2 teaspoon dried thyme
- 1/4 teaspoon dried rosemary
- 1/4 teaspoon garlic powder
- 1/4 teaspoon onion powder
- 1/4 teaspoon paprika
- Pinch of cayenne pepper (optional, for some heat)

35

Breakfast Burrito Bowl

Directions

- In a skillet over medium heat, add olive oil.
- Add cauliflower rice, cumin, garlic powder, salt, and pepper.
- Sauté for 5-7 minutes or until the cauliflower rice is tender and lightly browned.
- Set aside.
- In the same skillet, crack the eggs and cook to your liking (scrambled, fried, or poached).
- Season with salt and pepper.
- In a serving bowl, start with a layer of cauliflower rice.
- Add the cooked eggs on top of the cauliflower rice.
- Arrange avocado slices, cherry tomatoes, red onion, bell pepper, and black beans around the eggs.
- Drizzle salsa over the bowl.
- Garnish with fresh cilantro.
- Season with additional salt and pepper if desired.
- Serve immediately and enjoy your Primal Gourmet Breakfast Burrito Bowl!

Ingredients

For the Bowl:

- 2 large eggs
- 1/2 avocado, sliced
- 1/2 cup cherry tomatoes, halved
- 1/4 cup red onion, finely chopped
- 1/4 cup bell pepper, diced
- 1/4 cup black beans, drained and rinsed
- 1/4 cup salsa (look for one with no added sugars or preservatives)
- Fresh cilantro, chopped (for garnish)
- Salt and pepper to taste

For the Cauliflower Rice:

- 1 cup cauliflower rice (store-bought or homemade)
- 1 tablespoon olive oil
- 1/2 teaspoon ground cumin
- 1/2 teaspoon garlic powder
- Salt and pepper to taste

Mango Coconut Chia Pudding

Directions

- In a mixing bowl, combine the chia seeds and coconut milk.
- Stir well to ensure the chia seeds are evenly distributed in the milk.
- Let the mixture sit for about 5 minutes, stirring occasionally to prevent clumping.
- Add the honey or maple syrup (if using) to the chia mixture and stir.
- Mix in the vanilla extract and a pinch of salt to enhance the flavours.
- Cover the bowl and refrigerate the chia mixture for at least 4 hours or overnight.
- During this time, the chia seeds will absorb the liquid and create a thick, pudding-like consistency.
- While the chia pudding sets dice the ripe mango into small cubes.
- Once the chia pudding has reached the desired consistency, give it a good stir.
- Spoon a layer of the chia pudding into serving glasses or bowls.
- Add a layer of diced mango on top of the chia pudding.
- Continue layering the chia pudding and diced mango until the serving glasses are filled.
- Garnish the top with additional mango cubes or shredded coconut if desired.
- Serve chilled and enjoy your delicious Mango Coconut Chia Pudding!

Ingredients

- 1/4 cup chia seeds
- 1 cup coconut milk (full-fat for creaminess)
- 1 ripe mango, peeled and diced
- 1 tablespoon honey or maple syrup (optional, depending on sweetness preference)
- 1/2 teaspoon vanilla extract
- A pinch of salt

37

Frittata with Spinach and Feta

Directions

- Preheat your oven to 375°F (190°C).
- In a skillet, heat 1 tablespoon of olive oil over medium heat. Add the chopped red onion and cook until softened about 2-3 minutes.
- Add the chopped spinach to the skillet and sauté until wilted, about 1-2 minutes. Remove from heat and set aside
- In a mixing bowl, whisk the eggs until well beaten. Season with salt, pepper, and dried oregano.
- Add the sautéed spinach and red onion to the beaten eggs. Mix well.
- Gently fold in the crumbled feta cheese and halved cherry tomatoes.
- In an oven-safe skillet, heat the remaining 1 tablespoon of olive oil over medium heat.
- Pour the egg mixture into the skillet, ensuring an even distribution of ingredients.
- Allow the frittata to cook undisturbed for 3-4 minutes or until the edges begin to set.
- Transfer the skillet to the preheated oven and bake for 12-15 minutes or until the frittata is set in the centre and has a golden-brown top.
- Carefully remove the skillet from the oven. Allow the frittata to cool for a few minutes before slicing.
- Slice the frittata into wedges and serve warm.

Ingredients

- 8 large eggs
- 1 cup fresh spinach, chopped
- 1/2 cup feta cheese, crumbled
- 1/2 cup cherry tomatoes, halved
- 1/4 cup red onion, finely chopped
- 2 tablespoons olive oil
- 1 teaspoon dried oregano
- Salt and pepper to taste

Almond Flour Crepes with Mixed Berries

Directions

- In a blender, combine almond flour, eggs, almond milk, melted coconut oil, sweetener, vanilla extract, and a pinch of salt.
- Blend until the batter is smooth and well combined.
- Allow the batter to rest for about 10-15 minutes. This helps the crepes hold together better.
- Heat a non-stick skillet or crepe pan over medium heat. Lightly grease the pan with coconut oil or cooking spray.
- Pour a small amount of batter into the centre of the pan, swirling it around to spread thinly and evenly.
- Cook for about 1-2 minutes until the edges start to lift and the bottom is lightly golden. Flip and cook the other side for an additional 1-2 minutes.
- Repeat the process until all the batter is used.
- Lay each crepe flat on a serving plate.
- Place a generous handful of mixed berries in the centre of each crepe.
- Gently fold the sides of the crepe over the berries, creating a semi-circle or cylinder shape.
- Drizzle honey or maple syrup over the top and garnish with fresh mint leaves if desired.
- Serve immediately and enjoy your delicious Almond Flour Crepes with Mixed Berries!

Ingredients

For the Crepes:

- 1 cup almond flour
- 3 large eggs
- 1 cup almond milk (or any non-dairy milk of choice)
- 1 tablespoon melted coconut oil
- 1 tablespoon sweetener of choice (e.g., maple syrup or honey)
- 1 teaspoon vanilla extract
- A pinch of salt

For the Filling:

- 1 cup mixed berries (strawberries, blueberries, raspberries, etc.)
- 1 tablespoon honey or maple syrup (for drizzling)
- Fresh mint leaves for garnish (optional)

Avocado and Egg Breakfast Muffins

Directions

- Preheat your oven to 375°F (190°C).
- Carefully scoop out a small portion of the flesh from each avocado half to create a larger well for the egg.
- Place the avocado halves in a baking dish to keep them stable during baking.
- Crack one egg into each avocado half. Adjust the amount based on the size of your avocados.
- Sprinkle salt and pepper over each egg to taste.
- If desired, add toppings such as diced tomatoes, chives, or a sprinkle of shredded cheese on top of each egg.
- Carefully place the baking dish in the preheated oven and bake for about 15-20 minutes or until the eggs reach your desired level of doneness. Keep an eye on them to avoid overcooking.
- Once done, remove the avocado and egg muffins from the oven. Allow them to cool for a few minutes before serving.
- Serve the Avocado and Egg Breakfast Muffins warm.

Ingredients

- 2 avocados, halved and pitted
- 4 large eggs
- Salt and pepper, to taste
- Optional toppings: diced tomatoes, chives, shredded cheese

40

Smoothie with Kale, Pineapple, and Coconut Milk

Directions

- Wash the kale leaves thoroughly and remove the stems.
- Cut the pineapple into chunks.
- Peel and slice the banana.
- In a blender, combine the kale leaves, pineapple chunks, banana slices, coconut milk, and ice cubes.
- Optionally, add chia seeds for added texture and nutritional benefits.
- Start blending on low speed and gradually increase to high until the mixture is smooth and creamy.
- If the consistency is too thick, add water in small amounts until it reaches your desired thickness.
- Taste the smoothie and adjust the sweetness if necessary. Add honey or maple syrup if you prefer a sweeter taste.
- Pour the smoothie into a glass.
- Optionally, garnish with a pineapple wedge or a sprinkle of chia seeds.
- Stir the smoothie before sipping to ensure an even distribution of flavours.
- Enjoy your Primal Gourmet Green Smoothie as a refreshing and nutrient-packed beverage.

Ingredients

- 1 cup kale leaves, stems removed
- 1 cup fresh pineapple chunks
- 1/2 ripe banana
- 1/2 cup coconut milk (unsweetened)
- 1/2 cup ice cubes
- 1 tablespoon chia seeds (optional, for added texture and nutrients)
- 1 teaspoon honey or maple syrup (optional, for added sweetness)
- Water (as needed for desired consistency)

Banana Bread with Walnuts

Directions

- Preheat your oven to 350°F (175°C). Grease a standard-sized loaf pan with coconut oil or line it with parchment paper.
- In a large mixing bowl, mash the ripe bananas with a fork or potato masher until smooth.
- Add the eggs, melted coconut oil, honey or maple syrup, and vanilla extract to the mashed bananas. Mix well until all the wet ingredients are thoroughly combined.
- In a separate bowl, whisk together the almond flour, coconut flour, baking soda, and salt.
- Gradually add the dry ingredients to the wet ingredients, stirring continuously to ensure a smooth batter.
- Once the batter is well mixed, fold in the chopped walnuts.
- Pour the batter into the prepared loaf pan, spreading it evenly. If desired, sprinkle some extra chopped walnuts on top for added texture.
- Bake in the preheated oven for about 50-60 minutes or until a toothpick inserted into the center comes out clean.
- Allow the banana bread to cool in the pan for 10-15 minutes before transferring it to a wire rack to cool completely.
- Once cooled, slice the banana bread and enjoy! This banana bread can be served as is or with a spread of almond butter for an extra touch.

Ingredients

- 3 ripe bananas, mashed
- 3 large eggs
- 1/4 cup melted coconut oil
- 1/4 cup honey or maple syrup
- 1 teaspoon vanilla extract
- 2 cups almond flour
- 1/2 cup coconut flour
- 1 teaspoon baking soda
- 1/2 teaspoon salt
- 1/2 cup chopped walnuts (plus extra for topping)

Coconut Flour Pancakes with Almond Butter

Directions

- In a mixing bowl, whisk together the coconut flour, almond flour, baking powder, and a pinch of salt.
- In a separate bowl, beat the eggs and then add almond milk, melted coconut oil, and vanilla extract. Mix well.
- Slowly add the wet ingredients to the dry ingredients, stirring continuously to avoid lumps. If the batter is too thick, you can add a little more almond milk until you reach a pourable consistency.
- Optionally, sweeten the batter with maple syrup or honey to your liking.
- Heat a non-stick skillet or griddle over medium heat. Add a small amount of coconut oil to coat the surface.
- Spoon the batter onto the skillet, forming small pancakes. Cook for 2-3 minutes on one side until you see bubbles forming on the surface.
- Flip the pancakes and cook for an additional 1-2 minutes on the other side or until golden brown.
- Repeat until all the batter is used.
- Stack the pancakes on a plate.
- Spread almond butter on top of the pancakes.
- Optionally, drizzle with maple syrup and top with fresh berries.
- Serve the pancakes warm and enjoy the delightful combination of coconut flour goodness and the rich flavour of almond butter.

Ingredients

For the pancakes:

- 1/4 cup coconut flour
- 2 tablespoons almond flour
- 1/2 teaspoon baking powder
- Pinch of salt
- 3 large eggs
- 1/4 cup almond milk (or any milk of your choice)
- 1 tablespoon coconut oil, melted
- 1 teaspoon vanilla extract
- Optional: 1-2 tablespoons maple syrup or honey for sweetness

For serving:

- Almond butter
- Fresh berries (optional)
- Maple syrup (optional)

43

Almond Flour Waffles with Fresh Berries

Directions

- Preheat your waffle iron according to the manufacturer's instructions.
- In a large bowl, whisk together almond flour, coconut flour, baking powder, and salt until well combined.
- In a separate bowl, beat the eggs. Add almond milk, melted coconut oil (or butter), maple syrup (if using), and vanilla extract. Mix until well combined.
- Pour the wet ingredients into the bowl with the dry ingredients. Stir until a thick batter forms. Allow the batter to rest for a couple of minutes to let the coconut flour absorb some of the liquid.
- Lightly grease the waffle iron with coconut oil or non-stick cooking spray. Pour enough batter to cover the waffle iron, spreading it evenly.
- Close the waffle iron and cook until the waffles are golden brown and crisp. Cooking time may vary based on your waffle iron, usually around 4-5 minutes.
- Carefully remove the waffles from the iron and transfer them to a plate. Repeat the process with the remaining batter.
- Serve the almond flour waffles warm, topped with a generous portion of fresh berries. You can also add a drizzle of maple syrup, a dollop of yoghurt, or a sprinkle of chopped nuts if desired.

Ingredients

- 1 cup almond flour
- 2 tablespoons coconut flour
- 1 teaspoon baking powder
- 1/4 teaspoon salt
- 3 large eggs
- 1/4 cup unsweetened almond milk (or any milk of your choice)
- 2 tablespoons melted coconut oil (or butter)
- 1 tablespoon maple syrup or sweetener of choice (optional)
- 1 teaspoon vanilla extract
- Fresh berries for topping (strawberries, blueberries, raspberries, etc.)

Grilled Chicken Caesar Salad with Avocado Dressing

Directions

- Preheat the grill or a grill pan over medium-high heat.
- Season the chicken breasts with salt and black pepper.
- Drizzle olive oil over the chicken breasts, ensuring they are well-coated.
- Grill the chicken for 6-8 minutes per side or until the internal temperature reaches 165°F (74°C).
- Remove from the grill and let it rest for a few minutes before slicing.
- In a blender or food processor, combine the peeled and pitted avocado, olive oil, lemon juice, minced garlic, salt, black pepper, and Parmesan cheese (if using).
- Blend until smooth and creamy. If the dressing is too thick, you can thin it out with a bit of water or extra olive oil.
- In a large bowl, toss the chopped romaine lettuce with cherry tomatoes.
- Slice the grilled chicken breasts and arrange them on top of the salad.
- Drizzle the avocado dressing generously over the salad.
- Add croutons if desired, or use a primal-friendly alternative like roasted nuts for crunch.
- Serve the Grilled Chicken Caesar Salad immediately, ensuring the dressing evenly coats the salad.
- Garnish with additional Parmesan cheese, freshly ground black pepper, or a wedge of lemon for extra flavour.

Ingredients

For the Salad:

- 2 boneless, skinless chicken breasts
- Salt and black pepper to taste
- 1 tablespoon olive oil
- 1 head of romaine lettuce, washed and chopped
- 1 cup cherry tomatoes, halved
- 1/2 cup croutons (optional, or use a primal-friendly alternative)

For the Avocado Dressing:

- 1 ripe avocado, peeled and pitted
- 1/4 cup olive oil
- 2 tablespoons lemon juice
- 1 garlic clove, minced
- Salt and black pepper to taste
- 1/4 cup grated Parmesan cheese (optional)

Zucchini Noodles with Pesto and Cherry Tomatoes

Directions

- Use a spiralizer to create zucchini noodles. If you don't have a spiralizer, you can use a vegetable peeler to make thin ribbons.
- In a food processor, combine the basil, pine nuts, minced garlic, and Parmesan cheese. Pulse until the ingredients are finely chopped.
- With the food processor running, slowly stream in the olive oil until the pesto reaches your desired consistency. Season with salt and pepper to taste. If you like some heat, add red pepper flakes.
- In a large pan, heat a bit of olive oil over medium heat. Add the halved cherry tomatoes and sauté for 2-3 minutes until they just start to soften. You want them to maintain their shape.
- Add the zucchini noodles to the pan with the cherry tomatoes. Toss gently for 1-2 minutes, just until the zucchini noodles are slightly softened. Be careful not to overcook; you want them to have a bit of crunch.
- Add the prepared pesto to the pan with zucchini noodles and cherry tomatoes. Toss everything together until the noodles are evenly coated with the pesto.
- Remove from heat and garnish with additional fresh basil leaves. Optionally, sprinkle some extra Parmesan cheese and red pepper flakes for added flavour.
- This dish can be served warm or cold, depending on your preference. It makes a fantastic light lunch or a refreshing side dish for dinner.

Ingredients

- 4 medium-sized zucchinis, spiralized into noodles
- 1 cup cherry tomatoes, halved
- 1/2 cup fresh basil leaves, plus extra for garnish
- 1/4 cup pine nuts, toasted
- 2 cloves garlic, minced
- 1/2 cup freshly grated Parmesan cheese
- 1/2 cup extra-virgin olive oil
- Salt and pepper to taste
- Red pepper flakes (optional, for some heat)

Smoked Salmon and Avocado Cucumber Bites

Directions

- Wash the cucumber and slice it into rounds, about 1/4 inch thick. Place the cucumber rounds on a serving platter.
- Cut the ripe avocado in half, remove the pit, and scoop the flesh into a bowl.
- Mash the avocado with a fork until smooth.
- Add chopped dill, capers, red onion, and lemon juice to the mashed avocado.
- Season the mixture with salt and pepper to taste.
- Mix everything well to combine.
- Place a small spoonful of the avocado mixture on top of each cucumber round.
- Place a slice of smoked salmon on top of the avocado mixture on each cucumber round.
- Optional: Garnish each bite with additional dill, capers, or a squeeze of fresh lemon juice for extra flavour.
- Arrange the Smoked Salmon and Avocado Cucumber Bites on a serving platter and serve immediately.

Ingredients

- 1 English cucumber, sliced into rounds
- 8 oz smoked salmon, thinly sliced
- 1 ripe avocado
- 1 tablespoon fresh dill, chopped
- 1 tablespoon capers, drained
- 1 tablespoon red onion, finely chopped
- 1 tablespoon lemon juice
- Salt and pepper to taste

Chicken and Kale Stew with Turmeric

Directions

- In a bowl, season the chicken pieces with salt, black pepper, ground turmeric, ground cumin, paprika, and ground coriander. Toss well to coat the chicken evenly.
- Heat olive oil in a large pot over medium-high heat. Add the seasoned chicken pieces and scar them until browned on all sides. This step helps to lock in the flavour.
- Add the chopped onion to the pot and sauté until translucent. Add minced garlic and continue cooking for another minute until fragrant.
- Pour in the diced tomatoes with their juice. Stir well, scraping any browned bits from the bottom of the pot.
- Stir in the ground turmeric, ground cumin, paprika, and ground coriander. Mix the spices well with the other ingredients.
- Add the chicken broth to the pot, stirring to combine. Bring the mixture to a simmer.
- Add the sliced carrots and diced potatoes to the pot. Continue simmering until the vegetables start to soften.
- Once the vegetables are slightly tender, add the seared chicken back to the pot. Let the stew simmer over medium heat until the chicken is cooked through and the flavours meld together.
- About 10 minutes before serving, stir in the chopped kale. It will wilt into the stew as it cooks.
- Taste the stew and adjust the seasoning with salt and black pepper if needed.
- Ladle the Chicken and Kale Stew into bowls. Garnish with fresh cilantro or parsley if desired.

Ingredients

- 1.5 lbs boneless, skinless chicken thighs, cut into bite-sized pieces
- 1 tablespoon olive oil
- 1 onion, finely chopped
- 3 cloves garlic, minced
- 1 teaspoon ground turmeric
- 1 teaspoon ground cumin
- 1 teaspoon paprika
- 1/2 teaspoon ground coriander
- Salt and black pepper to taste
- 1 can (14 oz) diced tomatoes, undrained
- 4 cups chicken broth
- 2 carrots, peeled and sliced
- 2 potatoes, peeled and diced
- 4 cups fresh kale, stems removed and chopped
- Fresh cilantro or parsley for garnish (optional)

48

Eggplant and Portobello Mushroom Stack

Directions

- Preheat the oven to 400°F (200°C).
- Place the eggplant rounds on a baking sheet and sprinkle both sides with salt. Allow them to sit for about 15 minutes to draw out excess moisture. Afterwards, pat the eggplant slices dry with a paper towel.
- Preheat a grill or grill pan over medium-high heat.
- Brush the eggplant slices and Portobello mushrooms with olive oil and season with salt and pepper.
- Grill the eggplant for 3-4 minutes on each side or until tender. Grill the Portobello mushrooms for about 5-6 minutes per side, until they are cooked through and have grill marks.
- On a baking sheet, start assembling the stacks. Begin with a slice of grilled eggplant, followed by a Portobello mushroom, cherry tomatoes, and mozzarella.
- Repeat the layers until you have a stack of your desired height.
- Place the assembled stacks in the preheated oven for about 10-12 minutes, or until the mozzarella is melted and bubbly.
- While the stacks are baking, prepare the dressing. In a small bowl, whisk together minced garlic, chopped basil, balsamic vinegar, and the remaining olive oil. Season with salt and pepper to taste.
- Once the stacks are out of the oven, drizzle the balsamic dressing over the top.
- Optionally, drizzle with balsamic glaze for extra flavour.
- Serve immediately, garnished with additional fresh basil if desired.

Ingredients

- 1 large eggplant, sliced into 1/2-inch rounds
- 4 large Portobello mushrooms, stems removed
- 1 cup cherry tomatoes, halved
- 1 cup fresh mozzarella cheese, sliced
- 2 cloves garlic, minced
- 1/4 cup fresh basil leaves, chopped
- 2 tablespoons balsamic vinegar
- 3 tablespoons extra-virgin olive oil
- Salt and black pepper to taste
- Optional: Balsamic glaze for drizzling (optional)

49

Cabbage and Apple Slaw with Bison

Directions

- In a large bowl, combine the shredded green cabbage, red cabbage, apples, shredded carrots, and chopped cilantro.
- In a large skillet over medium heat, add olive oil. Add diced onions and cook until softened.
- Add minced garlic and ground bison to the skillet. Cook until the bison is browned and cooked through.
- Season the bison with ground cumin, smoked paprika, salt, and pepper. Stir well to incorporate the spices.
- In a small bowl, whisk together mayonnaise, apple cider vinegar, Dijon mustard, honey or maple syrup, salt, and pepper. Adjust the sweetness and acidity to your liking.
- Pour the dressing over the cabbage and apple mixture. Toss until the slaw is evenly coated with the dressing.
- Top the slaw with the cooked bison mixture. Toss gently to combine.
- Allow the flavours to meld for a few minutes before serving.
- Serve the Cabbage and Apple Slaw with Bison on its own as a satisfying salad or use it as a filling for lettuce wraps.
- For added crunch, sprinkle some toasted pumpkin seeds or chopped nuts on top.
- Garnish with extra cilantro or a squeeze of fresh lime juice before serving.

Ingredients

For the Slaw:
- 4 cups shredded green cabbage
- 2 cups shredded red cabbage
- 2 apples, thinly sliced (use your favourite variety)
- 1/2 cup shredded carrots
- 1/4 cup chopped fresh cilantro

For the Bison:
- 1 lb ground bison
- 1 tablespoon olive oil
- 1 small onion, finely diced
- 2 cloves garlic, minced
- 1 teaspoon ground cumin
- 1 teaspoon smoked paprika
- Salt and pepper to taste

For the Dressing:
- 1/4 cup mayonnaise (preferably homemade or a high-quality store-bought)
- 2 tablespoons apple cider vinegar
- 1 tablespoon Dijon mustard
- 1 tablespoon honey or maple syrup
- Salt and pepper to taste

Grilled Herb-Crusted Rack of Lamb with Asparagus

Directions

- In a small bowl, mix the chopped rosemary, thyme, minced garlic, Dijon mustard, olive oil, salt, and black pepper. This mixture will be the herb crust for the lamb.
- Preheat the grill to medium-high heat.
- Pat the racks of lamb dry with paper towels and season with salt and black pepper.
- Brush the lamb racks with the herb crust mixture, ensuring they are well-coated on all sides.
- Place the lamb racks on the preheated grill, bone side down.
- Grill for about 10-15 minutes, turning occasionally, or until the internal temperature reaches your desired level of doneness. For medium-rare, aim for an internal temperature of 135°F (57°C).
- Allow the lamb to rest for a few minutes before slicing.
- While the lamb is resting, toss the trimmed asparagus in olive oil, salt, and black pepper.
- Grill the asparagus on the hot grill for 5-7 minutes, or until they are tender and slightly charred.
- Sprinkle lemon zest over the grilled asparagus for a burst of freshness.
- Arrange the grilled herb-crusted rack of lamb on a serving platter.
- Serve the grilled asparagus alongside the lamb.
- Garnish with additional fresh herbs or lemon slices if desired.

Ingredients

For the Herb Crust:

- 2 racks of lamb, trimmed and frenched
- 3 tablespoons fresh rosemary, finely chopped
- 3 tablespoons fresh thyme, finely chopped
- 4 garlic cloves, minced
- 2 tablespoons Dijon mustard
- 2 tablespoons olive oil
- Salt and black pepper, to taste

For the Asparagus:

- 1 bunch of asparagus, trimmed
- 2 tablespoons olive oil
- Salt and black pepper, to taste
- Zest of 1 lemon

Tuna Salad Lettuce Wraps

Directions

- In a mixing bowl, combine the drained tuna, chopped celery, chopped red onion, mayonnaise, Dijon mustard, and fresh lemon juice.
- Mix the ingredients until well combined. The mayonnaise should coat the tuna evenly.
- Season the tuna salad with salt and pepper to taste. Adjust the seasoning according to your preferences.
- If desired, fold in the chopped fresh parsley for added freshness and flavour.
- To assemble the lettuce wraps, take a lettuce leaf, and spoon a generous portion of the tuna salad onto the center of the leaf.
- Gently fold the sides of the lettuce leaf over the tuna salad, creating a wrap or taco-like shape.
- Repeat the process with the remaining lettuce leaves and tuna salad.
- Serve immediately and enjoy your Tuna Salad Lettuce Wraps!

Optional Additions and Variations:
- **Avocado Slices:** Add creamy avocado slices for extra richness and texture.
- **Cherry Tomatoes:** Include halved cherry tomatoes for a burst of freshness.
- **Hot Sauce:** If you like a bit of heat, drizzle some hot sauce or sprinkle red pepper flakes into the tuna salad mixture.
- **Cucumber Strips:** Add thin cucumber strips for a cool crunch.

Ingredients

- 2 cans (about 10 oz each) of tuna, drained
- 1/2 cup mayonnaise (preferably homemade or a high-quality store-bought version)
- 1 celery stalk, finely chopped
- 1/4 red onion, finely chopped
- 1 tablespoon Dijon mustard
- 1 tablespoon fresh lemon juice
- Salt and pepper to taste
- 1-2 tablespoons fresh parsley, chopped (optional, for garnish)
- Butter lettuce leaves or large romaine leaves, washed and patted dry

Chicken Cobb Salad with Avocado

Directions

- Season the chicken breasts with salt and pepper.
- In a skillet over medium heat, add olive oil.
- Cook the chicken breasts for 5-7 minutes per side or until fully cooked.
- Allow the chicken to rest for a few minutes before slicing it into strips.
- In a small bowl, whisk together olive oil, red wine vinegar, Dijon mustard, honey, salt, and pepper. Set aside.
- In a large salad bowl, arrange the mixed greens as the base.
- Place the sliced chicken, cherry tomatoes, cucumber, red bell pepper, feta cheese, hard-boiled eggs, red onion, and crumbled bacon on top of the greens.
- Drizzle the dressing over the salad just before serving. Toss gently to coat the ingredients evenly.
- Add sliced avocados on top of the salad.
- Optionally, sprinkle chopped fresh parsley for added freshness.
- Serve the Chicken Cobb Salad with Avocado immediately, allowing everyone to mix their salad at the table.

Ingredients

For the Salad:

- 2 boneless, skinless chicken breasts
- Salt and pepper to taste
- 1 tablespoon olive oil
- 8 cups mixed salad greens (e.g., romaine lettuce, spinach)
- 1 cup cherry tomatoes, halved
- 1 cup cucumber, diced
- 1 cup red bell pepper, diced
- 1 cup crumbled feta cheese
- 4 hard-boiled eggs, sliced
- 1/2 cup red onion, thinly sliced
- 1/2 cup bacon, cooked and crumbled

For the Dressing:

- 1/4 cup olive oil
- 2 tablespoons red wine vinegar
- 1 teaspoon Dijon mustard
- 1 teaspoon honey
- Salt and pepper to taste

For Garnish:

- 2 ripe avocados, sliced
- Fresh parsley, chopped (optional)

53

Egg Salad Lettuce Wraps

Directions

- Place eggs in a single layer in a saucepan and cover with water.
- Bring water to a boil, then reduce heat to a simmer and cook for 9-10 minutes.
- Transfer eggs to an ice bath to cool, then peel and chop.
- In a mixing bowl, combine the chopped hard-boiled eggs, mayonnaise, Dijon mustard, chopped celery, chopped red onion, and chopped chives.
- Mix the ingredients until well combined, and the egg salad has a creamy consistency.
- Season the egg salad with salt and black pepper to taste. Adjust the seasoning according to your preference.
- Take a lettuce leaf and spoon a generous portion of the egg salad into the centre.
- Carefully fold or roll the lettuce leaf around the egg salad, creating a wrap or taco-like structure.
- Secure with a toothpick if needed.
- Repeat the process for the remaining lettuce leaves and egg salad.
- Arrange the Egg Salad Lettuce Wraps on a serving platter.
- Optionally, garnish with additional chopped chives or a sprinkle of paprika for colour.

Ingredients

- 6 hard-boiled eggs, peeled and chopped
- 1/4 cup mayonnaise (preferably homemade or high-quality store-bought)
- 1 tablespoon Dijon mustard
- 2 tablespoons finely chopped celery
- 2 tablespoons finely chopped red onion
- 1 tablespoon chopped fresh chives
- Salt and black pepper to taste
- Lettuce leaves (such as iceberg or butter lettuce) for wrapping

Asian-Inspired Chicken Salad

Directions

- In a bowl, mix soy sauce, hoisin sauce, sesame oil, minced ginger, and minced garlic.
- Place the chicken breasts in a shallow dish and pour the marinade over them. Let it marinate for at least 30 minutes.
- Preheat a grill or grill pan over medium-high heat.
- Grill the chicken breasts for 6-8 minutes per side or until fully cooked and no longer pink in the centre.
- Remove from the grill and let the chicken rest for a few minutes before slicing it into thin strips.
- In a large salad bowl, combine the mixed greens, shredded cabbage, shredded carrots, sliced red bell pepper, julienned cucumber, steamed edamame, green onions, and cilantro.
- In a small bowl, whisk together soy sauce, rice vinegar, sesame oil, honey or maple syrup, grated ginger, minced garlic, and sriracha sauce.
- Add the sliced chicken on top of the salad.
- Drizzle the dressing over the salad and toss everything together until well-coated.
- Sprinkle chopped cashews or peanuts on top for added crunch (optional).
- Serve immediately, and enjoy your Asian-Inspired Chicken Salad!

Ingredients

For the Chicken:
- 2 boneless, skinless chicken breasts
- 2 tablespoons soy sauce
- 1 tablespoon hoisin sauce
- 1 tablespoon sesame oil
- 1 teaspoon ginger, minced
- 1 teaspoon garlic, minced

For the Salad:
- 6 cups mixed salad greens (e.g., romaine, spinach, arugula)
- 1 cup shredded cabbage
- 1 cup shredded carrots
- 1 red bell pepper, thinly sliced
- 1 cucumber, julienned
- 1/2 cup edamame, steamed
- 1/4 cup green onions, sliced
- 1/4 cup cilantro, chopped
- 1/4 cup cashews or peanuts, chopped (optional, for garnish)

For the Dressing:
- 3 tablespoons soy sauce
- 2 tablespoons rice vinegar
- 1 tablespoon sesame oil
- 1 tablespoon honey or maple syrup
- 1 teaspoon ginger, grated
- 1 teaspoon garlic, minced
- 1 teaspoon sriracha sauce (adjust to taste)

Tuna and Avocado Salad

Directions

- Drain the canned tuna and transfer it to a large mixing bowl.
- Dice the ripe avocados, finely chop the red onion, dice the cucumber, and halve the cherry tomatoes.
- Add the diced avocados, chopped red onion, diced cucumber, cherry tomatoes, and chopped cilantro to the bowl with tuna.
- Squeeze the juice of one lemon over the salad.
- Drizzle extra-virgin olive oil over the ingredients.
- Season with salt and pepper to taste.
- Optional: Add a pinch of red pepper flakes for a hint of spiciness.
- Gently toss all the ingredients together until well combined, being careful not to mash the avocados.
- Divide the salad into individual servings and serve immediately.
- Customize the salad with additional ingredients like chopped fresh parsley, olives, or a sprinkle of feta cheese.
- Enjoy your refreshing and nutritious Tuna and Avocado Salad!

Ingredients

- 2 cans (about 10 oz each) of tuna, drained
- 2 ripe avocados, diced
- 1/2 red onion, finely chopped
- 1 cucumber, diced
- 1 cup cherry tomatoes, halved
- 1/4 cup fresh cilantro, chopped
- Juice of 1 lemon
- 2 tablespoons extra-virgin olive oil
- Salt and pepper to taste
- Optional: Red pepper flakes for a bit of heat

Tuna Poke Bowl with Cauliflower Rice

Directions

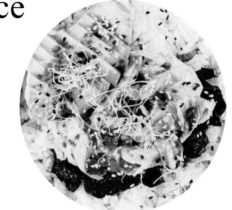

- In a bowl, combine soy sauce, sesame oil, rice vinegar, honey or maple syrup, grated ginger, minced garlic, and chopped green onion.
- Add diced tuna to the marinade and gently toss to coat. Let it marinate in the refrigerator for at least 15-20 minutes.
- Cut the cauliflower into florets and pulse in a food processor until it reaches a rice-like consistency.
- In a large skillet, heat coconut oil over medium heat. Add cauliflower rice and sauté for 5-7 minutes or until it's tender but not mushy. Season with salt and pepper.
- In serving bowls, start with a base of cauliflower rice.
- Arrange the marinated tuna on top of the cauliflower rice.
- Surround the tuna with mixed greens, cucumber slices, avocado, julienned carrots, and radishes.
- Sprinkle shredded nori seaweed over the bowl for a hint of umami.
- Garnish with sesame seeds and pickled ginger.
- Drizzle any remaining marinade over the bowl for extra flavour.
- Serve immediately and enjoy your Tuna Poke Bowl with Cauliflower Rice!

Ingredients

For the Tuna:
- 1 lb sushi-grade tuna, diced
- 2 tablespoons soy sauce (or tamari for a gluten-free option)
- 1 tablespoon sesame oil
- 1 teaspoon rice vinegar
- 1 teaspoon honey or maple syrup
- 1 teaspoon grated fresh ginger
- 1 clove garlic, minced
- 1 green onion, finely chopped
- Sesame seeds for garnish

For the Cauliflower Rice:
- 1 large head cauliflower, riced
- 1 tablespoon coconut oil
- Salt and pepper to taste

For the Bowl:
- 2 cups mixed greens (spinach, kale, or arugula)
- 1 cucumber, thinly sliced
- 1 avocado, sliced
- 1 carrot, julienned
- Radishes, thinly sliced (optional)
- Nori seaweed, shredded
- Pickled ginger for garnish

Mediterranean Quinoa Bowl with Grilled Vegetables

Directions

- In a medium saucepan, combine quinoa, water or vegetable broth, and salt.
- Bring to a boil, then reduce heat to low, cover, and simmer for about 15-20 minutes or until quinoa is cooked and water is absorbed.
- Fluff the quinoa with a fork and set aside.
- Preheat the grill or grill pan over medium-high heat.
- In a large bowl, toss the sliced zucchini, bell peppers, red onion, and cherry tomatoes with olive oil, minced garlic, dried oregano, salt, and black pepper.
- Grill the vegetables for 5-7 minutes, turning occasionally, until they have nice grill marks and are tender but still slightly crisp.
- Remove from the grill and set aside.
- In a small bowl, whisk together extra-virgin olive oil, balsamic vinegar, Dijon mustard, honey, minced garlic, salt, and black pepper. Adjust the seasoning to taste.
- In serving bowls, layer the cooked quinoa and grilled vegetables.
- Drizzle the Mediterranean dressing over the top.
- Add diced cucumber, sliced Kalamata olives, and crumbled feta cheese.
- Garnish with fresh chopped parsley.
- Serve the Mediterranean Quinoa Bowl with lemon wedges on the side for an extra burst of freshness.

Ingredients

For the Quinoa:
- 1 cup quinoa, rinsed and drained
- 2 cups water or vegetable broth
- 1/2 teaspoon salt

For the Grilled Vegetables:
- 1 zucchini, sliced
- 1 yellow bell pepper, sliced
- 1 red bell pepper, sliced
- 1 red onion, sliced
- 1 cup cherry tomatoes, halved
- 2 tablespoons olive oil
- 2 cloves garlic, minced
- 1 teaspoon dried oregano
- Salt and black pepper to taste

For the Mediterranean Dressing:
- 1/4 cup extra-virgin olive oil
- 2 tablespoons balsamic vinegar
- 1 teaspoon Dijon mustard
- 1 teaspoon honey
- 1 clove garlic, minced
- Salt and black pepper to taste

For the Assembly:
- 1 cup cucumber, diced
- 1/2 cup Kalamata olives, sliced
- 1/2 cup crumbled feta cheese
- Fresh parsley, chopped, for garnish
- Lemon wedges, for serving

Chicken Caesar Salad Wrap
with Lettuce

Directions

- In a bowl, whisk together mayonnaise, Dijon mustard, minced garlic, anchovy fillets (if using), Worcestershire sauce, lemon juice, and grated Parmesan cheese.
- Season with salt and black pepper to taste.
- Refrigerate the dressing while preparing the rest of the ingredients.
- Season the chicken breasts with salt, black pepper, and dried Italian seasoning.
- Heat olive oil in a grill pan or skillet over medium-high heat.
- Cook the chicken breasts for 6-8 minutes per side or until fully cooked.
- Allow the chicken to rest for a few minutes before slicing it into thin strips.
- Lay out a large Romaine lettuce leaf on a flat surface.
- Place a few slices of grilled chicken in the centre of the lettuce leaf.
- Add halved cherry tomatoes and a sprinkle of grated Parmesan cheese.
- Drizzle the Caesar dressing over the ingredients.
- Optionally, add croutons for an extra crunch.
- Fold the sides of the lettuce leaf over the filling.
- Starting from one end, roll the lettuce leaf to form a wrap.
- Secure with toothpicks if needed.
- Place the wrapped Chicken Caesar Salad on a serving plate.
- Serve with extra Caesar dressing on the side for dipping, if desired.

Ingredients

For the Caesar Dressing:

- 1/2 cup mayonnaise
- 2 tablespoons Dijon mustard
- 2 cloves garlic, minced
- 2 anchovy fillets, minced (optional)
- 1 tablespoon Worcestershire sauce
- 1 tablespoon fresh lemon juice
- 1/4 cup grated Parmesan cheese
- Salt and black pepper to taste

For the Chicken:

- 2 boneless, skinless chicken breasts
- Salt and black pepper to taste
- 1 tablespoon olive oil
- 1 teaspoon dried Italian seasoning

For the Salad:

- Romaine lettuce leaves, washed and dried
- Cherry tomatoes, halved
- Grated Parmesan cheese
- Croutons (optional)

Turkey and Avocado BLT Lettuce Wraps

Directions

- Carefully remove large, sturdy leaves from the head of lettuce. These will serve as the "wraps" for your BLTs.
- In a skillet over medium heat, cook the bacon until it's crispy. Once done, place it on paper towels to drain excess grease.
- Lay out the lettuce leaves on a clean surface.
- Spread a thin layer of mayonnaise on each lettuce leaf.
- Place a few slices of turkey on each lettuce leaf.
- Add slices of avocado, ensuring even distribution.
- Lay a slice of tomato on top.
- Break the crispy bacon into halves and place it on the stack.
- Sprinkle salt and pepper to taste over each wrap.
- In a small bowl, mix the Dijon mustard with a bit of mayonnaise. Drizzle this over the wraps for added flavour.
- If you like, add thinly sliced red onion for an extra kick.
- Carefully roll each lettuce leaf from one end to the other, creating a wrap.
- If needed, secure the wraps with toothpicks to hold them together.
- Arrange the Turkey and Avocado BLT Lettuce Wraps on a serving platter.
- Optionally, serve with an additional mustard-mayo mix on the side for dipping.

Ingredients

- 1 pound sliced turkey breast
- 8 large lettuce leaves (such as iceberg or butter lettuce)
- 1 large avocado, sliced
- 8 slices of bacon, cooked until crispy
- 1 large tomato, thinly sliced
- 1/4 cup mayonnaise
- 1 tablespoon Dijon mustard
- Salt and pepper, to taste
- Optional: Sliced red onion for added flavor

Waldorf Chicken Salad

Directions

For the Chicken:

- Preheat the oven to 375°F (190°C).
- Season the chicken breasts with salt and pepper on both sides.
- In an oven-safe skillet, heat olive oil over medium-high heat.
- Sear the chicken breasts for 2-3 minutes on each side until golden brown.
- Transfer the skillet to the preheated oven and bake for about 20-25 minutes or until the internal temperature of the chicken reaches 165°F (74°C).
- Remove from the oven, let it rest for a few minutes, then dice the chicken into bite-sized pieces.

For the Salad:

- In a large bowl, combine the diced chicken, apples, grapes, celery, and walnuts.
- In a small bowl, whisk together Greek yoghurt, mayonnaise, Dijon mustard, honey, salt, and pepper until well combined.
- Pour the dressing over the chicken and fruit mixture and gently toss until everything is evenly coated.
- Taste and adjust the seasoning if needed.
- Chill the Waldorf Chicken Salad in the refrigerator for at least 30 minutes to allow the flavours to meld.
- Before serving, garnish with chopped fresh parsley.

Serve the Waldorf Chicken Salad:

- Serve the Waldorf Chicken Salad on a bed of fresh greens, in lettuce cups, or between slices of your favourite bread for a delicious sandwich.

Ingredients

For the Chicken:

- 2 boneless, skinless chicken breasts
- Salt and pepper, to taste
- 1 tablespoon olive oil

For the Salad:

- 2 cups diced cooked chicken (from the roasted chicken)
- 2 apples, cored and diced (use a combination of sweet and tart apples)
- 1 cup red seedless grapes, halved
- 1 cup celery, thinly sliced
- 1/2 cup walnuts, toasted and chopped
- 1/2 cup Greek yogurt
- 2 tablespoons mayonnaise
- 1 tablespoon Dijon mustard
- 1 tablespoon honey
- Salt and pepper, to taste
- Fresh parsley, chopped (for garnish)

61

Caprese Stuffed Avocado

Directions

- Cut the avocados in half and remove the pits. Using a spoon, carefully scoop out a small amount of flesh from each avocado half to create a well for the stuffing. Place the avocado halves on a serving platter.
- In a mixing bowl, combine the cherry tomatoes, fresh mozzarella balls, and torn basil leaves.
- Spoon the Caprese mixture into the wells of the avocado halves, distributing it evenly among them
- Drizzle extra-virgin olive oil over the stuffed avocados, and then drizzle balsamic glaze for a sweet and tangy finish.
- Season the stuffed avocados with salt and pepper to taste. Adjust the seasoning according to your preferences.
- Serve the Caprese Stuffed Avocado immediately, garnished with additional fresh basil if desired.

Ingredients

- 2 ripe avocados, halved and pitted
- 1 cup cherry tomatoes, halved
- 1 cup fresh mozzarella balls (or diced mozzarella)
- 1/4 cup fresh basil leaves, torn
- 2 tablespoons extra-virgin olive oil
- 1 tablespoon balsamic glaze
- Salt and pepper, to taste

Greek Chicken Souvlaki with Tzatziki Sauce

Directions

- In a bowl, combine olive oil, minced garlic, dried oregano, thyme, rosemary, smoked paprika, lemon juice, salt, and pepper. Mix well to create the marinade.
- Add the chicken cubes to the marinade, ensuring each piece is well-coated. Cover the bowl and let it marinate in the refrigerator for at least 2 hours, or preferably overnight for maximum flavour.
- Preheat the grill or grill pan over medium-high heat.
- Thread the marinated chicken cubes onto the soaked wooden skewers.
- Grill the chicken skewers for 6-8 minutes, turning occasionally, until the chicken is cooked through and has a nice char.
- Remove the skewers from the grill and let them rest for a few minutes.

Tzatziki

- In a bowl, combine Greek yoghurt, grated and drained cucumber, minced garlic, chopped dill, chopped mint, olive oil, lemon juice, salt, and pepper. Mix well.
- Taste the tzatziki sauce and adjust the seasoning if necessary.
- Refrigerate the tzatziki sauce for at least 30 minutes to allow the flavours to meld.
- Serve the Greek Chicken Souvlaki on a platter with a side of Tzatziki Sauce for dipping. Optionally, serve with warm pita bread, sliced tomatoes, red onions, and a sprinkle of fresh herbs. Enjoy the delicious flavours of this classic Greek dish!

Ingredients

- 1.5 lbs boneless, skinless chicken breasts, cut into cubes
- 1/4 cup olive oil
- 3 cloves garlic, minced
- 1 teaspoon dried oregano
- 1 teaspoon dried thyme
- 1 teaspoon dried rosemary
- 1 teaspoon smoked paprika
- Juice of 1 lemon
- Salt and pepper to taste
- Wooden skewers, soaked in water for at least 30 minutes

Tzatziki Sauce:

- 1 cup Greek yogurt
- 1 cucumber, grated and drained
- 2 cloves garlic, minced
- 1 tablespoon fresh dill, chopped
- 1 tablespoon fresh mint, chopped
- 1 tablespoon olive oil
- 1 tablespoon lemon juice
- Salt and pepper to taste

63

Quinoa and Grilled Vegetable Bowl

Directions

- In a medium saucepan, combine the quinoa and water or vegetable broth. Bring to a boil, then reduce the heat to low, cover, and simmer for 15-20 minutes, or until the quinoa is cooked and the liquid is absorbed. Fluff with a fork and set aside.
- Preheat your grill to medium-high heat.
- In a large bowl, toss the sliced zucchini, yellow squash, red bell pepper, yellow bell pepper, and red onion with olive oil, minced garlic, dried oregano, salt, and pepper.
- Place the marinated vegetables on the preheated grill. Grill for about 5-7 minutes per side or until the vegetables are tender and have nice grill marks.
- In serving bowls, layer the cooked quinoa and grilled vegetables.
- Drizzle fresh lemon juice over the quinoa and vegetables to add a bright, citrusy flavour.
- Sprinkle chopped fresh parsley and crumbled feta cheese (if using) over the top for added flavour and freshness.
- Serve the quinoa and grilled vegetable bowl warm, optionally with lemon wedges on the side for extra zest.

Ingredients

- 1 cup quinoa, rinsed and drained
- 2 cups water or vegetable broth
- 1 medium zucchini, sliced
- 1 medium yellow squash, sliced
- 1 red bell pepper, sliced
- 1 yellow bell pepper, sliced
- 1 red onion, sliced
- 2 tablespoons olive oil
- 2 cloves garlic, minced
- 1 teaspoon dried oregano
- Salt and pepper to taste
- 2 tablespoons fresh lemon juice
- 1/4 cup fresh parsley, chopped
- 1/4 cup feta cheese, crumbled (optional)
- Lemon wedges for serving

Shrimp and Mango Salad

Directions

- In a large pot of boiling water, cook the shrimp for 2-3 minutes until they turn pink and opaque. Drain and let them cool.
- In a large salad bowl, combine the cooked shrimp, diced mangoes, sliced cucumber, sliced red bell pepper, chopped red onion, and fresh cilantro.
- In a small bowl, whisk together the olive oil, lime juice, honey or maple syrup, Dijon mustard, salt, and pepper until well combined.
- Drizzle the dressing over the salad ingredients.
- Gently toss the salad until the ingredients are well coated with the dressing.
- Place the salad in the refrigerator for about 30 minutes to allow the flavours to meld.
- Once chilled, serve the shrimp and mango salad on a platter or individual plates.
- Garnish with additional cilantro leaves or lime wedges if desired.

Ingredients

For the Salad:

- 1 pound large shrimp, peeled and deveined
- 2 ripe mangoes, peeled, pitted, and diced
- 1 cucumber, thinly sliced
- 1 red bell pepper, thinly sliced
- 1/4 cup red onion, finely chopped
- 1/4 cup fresh cilantro, chopped

For the Dressing:

- 3 tablespoons olive oil
- 2 tablespoons lime juice
- 1 tablespoon honey or maple syrup
- 1 teaspoon Dijon mustard
- Salt and pepper to taste

Spinach and Strawberry Salad with Grilled Chicken

Directions

- Season the chicken breasts with salt and pepper.
- Preheat the grill or grill pan over medium-high heat.
- Grill the chicken breasts for 6-8 minutes per side or until fully cooked and grill marks appear.
- Allow the chicken to rest for a few minutes, then slice it into thin strips.
- In a dry skillet over medium heat, toast the sliced almonds until golden brown and fragrant. Keep a close eye on them, as they can burn quickly. Set aside to cool.
- In a large bowl, combine the baby spinach, sliced strawberries, and grilled chicken strips.
- Sprinkle the toasted almonds over the salad.
- If using, add the crumbled feta cheese for an extra layer of flavour.
- In a small bowl, whisk together the olive oil, balsamic vinegar, honey, and Dijon mustard until well combined.
- Season with salt and black pepper to taste.
- Drizzle the dressing over the salad just before serving. Toss gently to coat the ingredients evenly.
- Divide the salad among individual plates or serve it family-style on a large platter.

Ingredients

For the Salad:

- 2 boneless, skinless chicken breasts
- Salt and black pepper to taste
- 6 cups fresh baby spinach leaves, washed and dried
- 1 cup strawberries, hulled and sliced
- 1/2 cup sliced almonds, toasted
- 1/4 cup crumbled feta cheese (optional)

For the Dressing:

- 3 tablespoons extra-virgin olive oil
- 2 tablespoons balsamic vinegar
- 1 tablespoon honey
- 1 teaspoon Dijon mustard
- Salt and black pepper to taste

66

Thai-Inspired Beef Salad with Mint and Cilantro

Directions

- In a bowl, whisk together the soy sauce, fish sauce, lime juice, honey, minced garlic, grated ginger, and sesame oil.
- Add the thinly sliced flank steak to the marinade, ensuring it's well-coated. Cover and refrigerate for at least 30 minutes to allow the flavours to meld.
- In a large salad bowl, combine the mixed greens, cucumber slices, red bell pepper slices, julienned carrot, sliced red onion, chopped mint leaves, and chopped cilantro.
- Preheat a grill or grill pan over medium-high heat.
- Grill the marinated flank steak for 2-3 minutes per side or until it reaches the desired level of doneness. Remove from the grill and let it rest for a few minutes.
- Thinly slice the grilled flank steak against the grain.
- Arrange the sliced beef on top of the prepared salad.
- In a small bowl, whisk together the soy sauce, fish sauce, lime juice, honey, rice vinegar, sesame oil, and chilli paste.
- Drizzle the dressing over the salad and beef. Toss gently to combine, ensuring the salad is evenly coated with the dressing.
- Garnish the Thai-inspired beef salad with chopped roasted peanuts (if using).
- Serve immediately, with lime wedges on the side for an extra burst of citrus flavor.

Ingredients

For the Beef Marinade:
- 1 pound (450g) flank steak, thinly sliced
- 3 tablespoons soy sauce
- 2 tablespoons fish sauce
- 2 tablespoons lime juice
- 1 tablespoon honey
- 2 cloves garlic, minced
- 1 teaspoon ginger, grated
- 1 teaspoon sesame oil

For the Salad:
- 6 cups mixed salad greens (lettuce, spinach, arugula)
- 1 cucumber, thinly sliced
- 1 red bell pepper, thinly sliced
- 1 carrot, julienned
- 1/2 red onion, thinly sliced
- 1/2 cup fresh mint leaves, chopped
- 1/2 cup fresh cilantro leaves, chopped
- 1/4 cup roasted peanuts, chopped (optional, for garnish)
- Lime wedges, for serving

For the Dressing:
- 3 tablespoons soy sauce
- 2 tablespoons fish sauce
- 2 tablespoons lime juice
- 1 tablespoon honey
- 1 tablespoon rice vinegar
- 1 tablespoon sesame oil
- 1 teaspoon chili paste (adjust to taste)

Greek Salad with Grilled Chicken

Directions

- In a bowl, mix olive oil, dried oregano, dried thyme, salt, black pepper, and lemon juice.
- Place chicken breasts in a resealable plastic bag and pour the marinade over them. Seal the bag and let it marinate in the refrigerator for at least 30 minutes.
- Preheat your grill to medium-high heat.
- Remove the chicken from the marinade and grill for about 6-8 minutes per side or until the internal temperature reaches 165°F (74°C).
- Allow the chicken to rest for a few minutes before slicing it into strips.
- In a large salad bowl, combine cherry tomatoes, cucumber, red bell pepper, red onion, Kalamata olives, and feta cheese.
- In a small bowl, whisk together extra-virgin olive oil, red wine vinegar, Dijon mustard, minced garlic, dried oregano, salt, and black pepper.
- Add the grilled chicken strips to the salad.
- Drizzle the dressing over the salad and gently toss to combine, ensuring the salad is evenly coated with the dressing.
- Divide the Greek Salad with Grilled Chicken among serving plates.
- Optionally, garnish with additional feta cheese and a sprinkle of fresh oregano.

Ingredients

For the Grilled Chicken:

- 2 boneless, skinless chicken breasts
- 2 tablespoons olive oil
- 1 teaspoon dried oregano
- 1 teaspoon dried thyme
- Salt and black pepper to taste
- Juice of 1 lemon

For the Salad:

- 2 cups cherry tomatoes, halved
- 1 cucumber, diced
- 1 red bell pepper, diced
- 1/2 red onion, thinly sliced
- 1 cup Kalamata olives, pitted
- 1 cup feta cheese, crumbled

For the Dressing:

- 1/4 cup extra-virgin olive oil
- 2 tablespoons red wine vinegar
- 1 teaspoon Dijon mustard
- 1 clove garlic, minced
- 1 teaspoon dried oregano
- Salt and black pepper to taste

Shrimp and Avocado Salad

Directions

- In a large pot of boiling salted water, cook the shrimp for 2-3 minutes until they turn pink and opaque. Be careful not to overcook. Drain and let them cool.
- In a small bowl, whisk together lime juice, olive oil, salt, and pepper to create the dressing.
- In a large mixing bowl, combine the cooked shrimp, diced avocados, cherry tomatoes, red onion, and chopped cilantro.
- Pour the dressing over the shrimp and avocado mixture. Gently toss everything together until well coated.
- If desired, serve the shrimp and avocado salad over a bed of mixed salad greens for added freshness and crunch.
- For enhanced flavours, refrigerate the salad for 30 minutes before serving. This allows the ingredients to marinate and meld together.
- Garnish with additional cilantro or a wedge of lime before serving.
- Serve the shrimp and avocado salad as a light and refreshing meal. It's perfect for lunch, dinner, or as a side dish for a summer barbecue.

Ingredients

- 1 lb large shrimp, peeled and deveined
- 2 avocados, diced
- 1 cup cherry tomatoes, halved
- 1/4 cup red onion, finely chopped
- 1/4 cup fresh cilantro, chopped
- Juice of 2 limes
- 2 tablespoons olive oil
- Salt and pepper, to taste
- Mixed salad greens (optional, for serving)

69

Chicken and Vegetable Kebabs with Tzatziki Sauce

Directions

- In a bowl, combine the chicken cubes with olive oil, lemon juice, garlic powder, dried oregano, salt, and pepper. Mix well and let it marinate for at least 30 minutes, or refrigerate for a few hours for enhanced flavour.
- Thread the marinated chicken, bell peppers, red onion, zucchini, and cherry tomatoes onto the skewers, alternating the ingredients.
- Preheat the grill to medium-high heat. Grill the kebabs for about 12-15 minutes, turning occasionally, until the chicken is cooked through and the vegetables are tender and slightly charred.

Tzatziki

- If using a seeded cucumber, scoop out the seeds and finely chop the cucumber.
- In a bowl, combine Greek yoghurt, chopped cucumber, minced garlic, fresh dill, fresh mint (if using), olive oil, and lemon juice. Mix well.
- Season the tzatziki sauce with salt and pepper to taste. Refrigerate for at least 30 minutes to allow the flavours to meld.
- Serve the grilled chicken and vegetable kebabs hot off the grill, drizzled with the refreshing tzatziki sauce.

Ingredients

- 1.5 lbs boneless, skinless chicken breasts, cut into 1-inch cubes
- 1 large red bell pepper, cut into chunks
- 1 large yellow bell pepper, cut into chunks
- 1 red onion, cut into chunks
- 1 zucchini, sliced into rounds
- Cherry tomatoes
- Olive oil
- Lemon juice
- Garlic powder
- Dried oregano
- Wooden or metal skewers

Tzatziki Sauce

- 1 cup Greek yogurt
- 1/2 cucumber, peeled, seeded, and finely chopped
- 2 cloves garlic, minced
- 1 tablespoon fresh dill, chopped
- 1 tablespoon fresh mint, chopped (optional)
- 1 tablespoon olive oil
- 1 teaspoon lemon juice

Roasted Vegetable Salad with Balsamic Glaze

Directions

- Preheat your oven to 400°F (200°C).
- In a large mixing bowl, combine the cherry tomatoes, zucchini, yellow bell pepper, red bell pepper, and red onion.
- Drizzle olive oil over the vegetables and toss to coat evenly.
- Season with salt and pepper to taste.
- Spread the vegetables evenly on a baking sheet lined with parchment paper.
- Roast in the preheated oven for about 20-25 minutes or until the vegetables are tender and slightly caramelized. Make sure to toss the vegetables halfway through the roasting time for even cooking.
- In a small saucepan, combine balsamic vinegar, honey or maple syrup, minced garlic, salt, and pepper.
- Bring the mixture to a simmer over medium heat.
- Reduce the heat to low and let it simmer for 10-15 minutes or until the glaze thickens. Stir occasionally to prevent burning.
- In a large salad bowl, place the mixed salad greens.
- Add the roasted vegetables on top of the greens.
- Drizzle the balsamic glaze over the salad.
- Toss gently to combine, ensuring the vegetables are well coated with the glaze.
- Garnish the salad with crumbled feta cheese (if using) and chopped fresh basil.
- Serve the roasted vegetable salad immediately, and enjoy the delicious combination of flavours and textures.

Ingredients

For the Salad:

- 2 cups cherry tomatoes, halved
- 1 medium zucchini, sliced
- 1 medium yellow bell pepper, sliced
- 1 medium red bell pepper, sliced
- 1 red onion, sliced
- 2 tablespoons olive oil
- Salt and pepper to taste
- 4 cups mixed salad greens (arugula, spinach, or your choice)
- 1/2 cup crumbled feta cheese (optional)
- 1/4 cup chopped fresh basil leaves

For the Balsamic Glaze:

- 1/2 cup balsamic vinegar
- 2 tablespoons honey or maple syrup
- 1 clove garlic, minced
- Salt and pepper to taste

Caprese Salad with Grilled Chicken

Directions

- Season the chicken breasts with salt and pepper.
- Preheat the grill or grill pan over medium-high heat.
- Grill the chicken breasts for 6-8 minutes per side or until fully cooked and grill marks appear.
- Allow the chicken to rest for a few minutes, then slice it into thin strips.
- In a dry skillet over medium heat, toast the sliced almonds until golden brown and fragrant. Keep a close eye on them, as they can burn quickly. Set aside to cool.
- In a large bowl, combine the baby spinach, sliced strawberries, and grilled chicken strips.
- Sprinkle the toasted almonds over the salad.
- If using, add the crumbled feta cheese for an extra layer of flavour.
- In a small bowl, whisk together the olive oil, balsamic vinegar, honey, and Dijon mustard until well combined.
- Season with salt and black pepper to taste.
- Drizzle the dressing over the salad just before serving. Toss gently to coat the ingredients evenly.
- Divide the salad among individual plates or serve it family-style on a large platter.

Ingredients

For the Salad:

- 2 boneless, skinless chicken breasts
- Salt and pepper, to taste
- 2 tablespoons olive oil
- 1 teaspoon Italian seasoning (or a mix of dried basil, oregano, and thyme)
- 1 cup cherry tomatoes, halved
- 1 ball fresh mozzarella cheese, sliced
- Fresh basil leaves, torn
- Balsamic glaze, for drizzling

For the Dressing:

- 3 tablespoons extra virgin olive oil
- 1 tablespoon balsamic vinegar
- Salt and pepper, to taste

Turkey and Vegetable Skewers with Chimichurri Sauce

Directions

- In a bowl, mix the olive oil, minced garlic, smoked paprika, ground cumin, salt, and black pepper.
- Add the turkey cubes to the marinade, ensuring each piece is well-coated. Cover the bowl and let it marinate in the refrigerator for at least 30 minutes.
- In a separate bowl, combine chopped parsley, chopped cilantro, minced garlic, extra virgin olive oil, red wine vinegar, dried oregano, salt, black pepper, and red pepper flakes (if using).
- Mix well and let the flavours meld while you prepare the skewers.
- Preheat the grill or grill pan over medium-high heat.
- Thread the marinated turkey cubes, bell peppers, red onion, zucchini slices, and cherry tomatoes onto skewers, alternating the ingredients.
- Place the skewers on the preheated grill and cook for about 10-12 minutes, turning occasionally, until the turkey is cooked through and the vegetables are slightly charred.
- Remove the skewers from the grill and place them on a serving platter.
- Drizzle the chimichurri sauce over the skewers or serve it on the side for dipping.
- Serve the Turkey and Vegetable Skewers with Chimichurri Sauce over a bed of quinoa, rice, or your favourite grain. Garnish with additional fresh herbs if desired.

Ingredients

For the Skewers:

- 1 pound turkey breast, cut into bite-sized cubes
- 1 red bell pepper, cut into chunks
- 1 yellow bell pepper, cut into chunks
- 1 red onion, cut into chunks
- 1 zucchini, sliced into rounds
- Cherry tomatoes

For the Marinade:

- 3 tablespoons olive oil
- 2 cloves garlic, minced
- 1 teaspoon smoked paprika
- 1 teaspoon ground cumin
- Salt and black pepper, to taste

For Chimichurri Sauce:

- 1 cup fresh parsley, finely chopped
- 1/2 cup fresh cilantro, finely chopped
- 3 cloves garlic, minced
- 1/2 cup extra virgin olive oil
- 2 tablespoons red wine vinegar
- 1 teaspoon dried oregano
- Salt and black pepper, to taste
- Red pepper flakes (optional, for heat)

Beef and Vegetable Bone Broth Soup

Directions

- Preheat the oven to 400°F (200°C).
- Place the beef marrow bones on a baking sheet and roast in the oven for about 30 minutes, or until they develop a golden brown colour. This step enhances the flavour of the broth.
- In a large stockpot, combine the roasted beef bones, quartered onion, chopped carrots, celery, smashed garlic, leek, bay leaf, black peppercorns, thyme, and parsley.
- Add 8 cups of water to the pot, ensuring that the ingredients are fully submerged.
- Bring the mixture to a boil, then reduce the heat to low and let it simmer for at least 4 hours, or ideally up to 24 hours. The longer it simmers, the richer the flavour will be.
- Periodically skim off any foam or impurities that rise to the surface during the simmering process.
- Once the broth has simmered to your satisfaction, strain it through a fine mesh sieve or cheesecloth into another large pot or bowl. Discard the solids.
- Season the broth with salt to taste. Start with a small amount and add more if needed.
- Ladle the hot beef and vegetable bone broth into bowls. Optionally, garnish with chopped fresh herbs such as parsley or thyme.
- Allow any leftover broth to cool before storing it in airtight containers. It can be refrigerated for up to a week or frozen for longer storage.

Ingredients

- 2 pounds beef marrow bones
- 1 onion, quartered
- 2 carrots, chopped
- 2 celery stalks, chopped
- 4 cloves garlic, smashed
- 1 leek, chopped
- 1 bay leaf
- 1 teaspoon black peppercorns
- 2 sprigs fresh thyme
- 1 bunch parsley
- 8 cups water
- Salt, to taste
- Chopped fresh herbs for garnish (optional)

Grilled Lemon Garlic Herb Chicken with Cauliflower Mash

Directions

- In a bowl, mix the lemon juice, minced garlic, chopped herbs, olive oil, salt, and pepper to create the marinade.
- Place the chicken breasts in a zip-top bag or shallow dish and pour the marinade over them. Ensure that the chicken is well-coated. Marinate in the refrigerator for at least 30 minutes, or preferably a few hours for the flavours to meld.
- Preheat the grill to medium-high heat.
- Remove the chicken from the marinade and let any excess drip off. Reserve the marinade for basting.
- Grill the chicken breasts for about 6-8 minutes per side, or until the internal temperature reaches 165°F (74°C) and the chicken is no longer pink in the centre.
- While grilling, baste the chicken with the reserved marinade for added flavour.
- Once cooked, let the chicken rest for a few minutes before serving.

Cauliflower Mash:
- Steam or boil the cauliflower until fork-tender, approximately 10-12 minutes.
- In a pan, melt the butter or ghee over medium heat. Add the minced garlic and sauté for 1-2 minutes until fragrant.
- Transfer the steamed cauliflower to a food processor or blender. Add the garlic-infused butter, salt, and pepper.
- Blend until smooth and creamy, adjusting the seasoning to taste.
- Serve the Grilled Lemon Garlic Herb Chicken on a bed of cauliflower mash, garnished with fresh chives if desired.

Ingredients

- 4 boneless, skinless chicken breasts
- 2 lemons, juiced
- 4 cloves garlic, minced
- 2 tablespoons fresh herbs (such as rosemary, thyme, or oregano), chopped
- 2 tablespoons olive oil
- Salt and pepper to taste

Cauliflower Mash:
- 1 large head of cauliflower, cut into florets
- 2 tablespoons butter or ghee
- 2 cloves garlic, minced
- Salt and pepper to taste
- Fresh chives for garnish (optional)

75

Spicy Butternut Squash Soup

Directions

- Preheat the oven to 400°F (200°C).
- On a large baking sheet, toss the diced butternut squash, chopped onion, carrots, and minced garlic with olive oil.
- Spread the vegetables in a single layer and roast in the preheated oven for about 25-30 minutes or until the vegetables are tender and slightly caramelized.
- In a large pot, transfer the roasted vegetables and add chopped apple, ground cumin, ground coriander, smoked paprika, cayenne pepper, salt, and black pepper.
- Pour in the vegetable broth and bring the mixture to a simmer. Let it cook for about 15-20 minutes to allow the flavours to meld.
- Use an immersion blender or transfer the soup in batches to a blender to puree until smooth. If using a blender, be cautious with hot liquids and blend in batches to avoid splattering.
- If the soup is too thick, add more vegetable broth until you reach your desired consistency. If you prefer a creamier soup, stir in coconut milk.
- Taste the soup and adjust the seasoning, adding more salt, pepper, or cayenne pepper if needed.
- Ladle the hot soup into bowls and garnish with fresh cilantro or parsley.
- Serve the Spicy Butternut Squash Soup hot, perhaps with a slice of crusty bread or a dollop of Greek yogurt if desired.

Ingredients

- 1 medium-sized butternut squash, peeled, seeded, and diced
- 1 large onion, chopped
- 2 carrots, peeled and chopped
- 2 cloves garlic, minced
- 1 apple, peeled, cored, and chopped
- 4 cups vegetable broth
- 1 teaspoon ground cumin
- 1/2 teaspoon ground coriander
- 1/2 teaspoon smoked paprika
- 1/4 teaspoon cayenne pepper (adjust to taste for desired spice level)
- Salt and black pepper to taste
- 2 tablespoons olive oil
- 1 cup coconut milk (optional, for creaminess)
- Fresh cilantro or parsley for garnish

Bison and Sweet Potato Sliders

Directions

- Grate the peeled sweet potato using a box grater. Place the grated sweet potato in a clean kitchen towel and squeeze out any excess moisture.
- In a large mixing bowl, combine the ground bison, grated sweet potato, chopped onion, minced garlic, dried oregano, smoked paprika, salt, and pepper. Use your hands to mix the ingredients thoroughly.
- Divide the mixture into small portions and shape them into slider-sized patties. Ensure that the patties are of uniform thickness for even cooking.
- Heat a skillet or grill pan over medium heat and add a drizzle of olive oil.
- Cook the sliders for about 3-4 minutes per side, or until they reach your desired level of doneness. Bison is lean meat, so be cautious not to overcook them to keep them moist.
- Toast the slider buns or prepare lettuce wraps.
- Place each cooked slider on a bun or lettuce leaf.
- Add your favourite toppings, such as lettuce, tomato slices, avocado, or any condiments of your choice.
- Arrange the sliders on a serving platter and serve immediately.

Ingredients

- 1 pound ground bison
- 1 large sweet potato, peeled and grated
- 1 small onion, finely chopped
- 2 cloves garlic, minced
- 1 teaspoon dried oregano
- 1 teaspoon smoked paprika
- Salt and pepper, to taste
- Olive oil, for cooking
- Slider buns or lettuce wraps
- Toppings of your choice (lettuce, tomato, avocado, etc.)

Seared Salmon with Dill Sauce

Directions

- In a bowl, combine Greek yoghurt, mayonnaise, chopped dill, Dijon mustard, minced garlic, salt, and pepper.
- Mix well until all ingredients are thoroughly combined.
- Taste the sauce and adjust the seasoning if necessary.
- Add lemon juice to achieve the desired level of acidity. Set aside.
- Pat the salmon fillets dry with paper towels to remove excess moisture.
- Season both sides of each fillet with salt and pepper.
- Heat olive oil in a large skillet over medium-high heat.
- Once the oil is hot, carefully place the salmon fillets in the skillet, skin side down.
- Sear the salmon for about 3-4 minutes on each side, or until the skin is crispy and the salmon is cooked to your liking. Adjust cooking time based on the thickness of the fillets.
- Place the seared salmon fillets on a serving plate.
- Spoon a generous amount of the dill sauce over each fillet.
- Garnish with lemon slices.
- Serve immediately, and enjoy your Seared Salmon with Dill Sauce!

Ingredients

For the Salmon:
- 4 salmon fillets, skin-on
- Salt and pepper to taste
- 2 tablespoons olive oil
- 1 lemon, sliced (for garnish)

For the Dill Sauce:
- 1/2 cup Greek yogurt
- 2 tablespoons mayonnaise
- 2 tablespoons fresh dill, chopped
- 1 tablespoon Dijon mustard
- 1 clove garlic, minced
- Salt and pepper to taste
- Lemon juice to taste

Roasted Brussels Sprouts

Directions

- Preheat your oven to 400°F (200°C).
- Trim the ends of the Brussels sprouts and cut them in half. Remove any loose or yellowed outer leaves.
- In a large bowl, toss the Brussels sprouts with olive oil, minced garlic, sea salt, and black pepper until well coated.
- Spread the Brussels sprouts in a single layer on a baking sheet. Make sure they are evenly spaced to allow for even roasting.
- Roast the Brussels sprouts in the preheated oven for 20-25 minutes or until they are golden brown and crispy on the edges. Toss the Brussels sprouts halfway through the cooking time for even browning.
- If desired, drizzle the roasted Brussels sprouts with balsamic glaze for added flavour. You can also sprinkle grated Parmesan cheese over the top before serving.
- Transfer the roasted Brussels sprouts to a serving dish and serve them warm. They make a fantastic side dish for various meals.
- Enjoy the crispy, caramelized goodness of the roasted Brussels sprouts!

Ingredients

- 1 pound Brussels sprouts, trimmed and halved
- 2 tablespoons olive oil
- 2 cloves garlic, minced
- 1 teaspoon sea salt
- 1/2 teaspoon black pepper
- Optional: 1-2 tablespoons balsamic glaze for drizzling (after roasting)
- Optional: Grated Parmesan cheese for serving

Lemon Herb Grilled Shrimp Skewers

Directions

- If using wooden skewers, soak them in water for about 30 minutes to prevent burning on the grill.
- In a bowl, combine olive oil, minced garlic, lemon zest, lemon juice, dried oregano, dried thyme, dried rosemary, salt, and black pepper. Mix well to create the marinade.
- Add the peeled and deveined shrimp to the marinade, making sure each shrimp is well-coated. Cover the bowl and refrigerate for at least 30 minutes to allow the flavours to meld.
- Preheat the grill to medium-high heat.
- Thread the marinated shrimp onto the skewers, making sure to leave space between each shrimp.
- Place the shrimp skewers on the preheated grill. Grill for 2-3 minutes per side, or until the shrimp are opaque and have grill marks.
- Baste the shrimp with any remaining marinade during the grilling process for added flavour.
- Once the shrimp are cooked through, remove them from the grill and serve immediately.
- Garnish with additional lemon wedges and fresh herbs if desired.
- Enjoy your Lemon Herb Grilled Shrimp Skewers with a side of your favourite grilled vegetables or a light salad.

Ingredients

- 1 pound large shrimp, peeled and deveined
- 3 tablespoons olive oil
- 3 cloves garlic, minced
- Zest of 1 lemon
- Juice of 1 lemon
- 1 teaspoon dried oregano
- 1 teaspoon dried thyme
- 1 teaspoon dried rosemary
- Salt and black pepper to taste
- Wooden or metal skewers

Sesame Ginger Glazed Salmon

Directions

- In a small bowl, whisk together soy sauce, sesame oil, rice vinegar, minced ginger, minced garlic, and honey (or maple syrup). This creates a flavorful glaze for the salmon.
- Place the salmon fillets in a shallow dish or a resealable plastic bag.
- Pour half of the glaze over the salmon, making sure each fillet is well-coated. Reserve the other half of the glaze for later use.
- Allow the salmon to marinate for at least 15-30 minutes, allowing the flavours to infuse into the fish.
- Preheat your oven to 400°F (200°C).
- Place the marinated salmon fillets on a baking sheet lined with parchment paper or lightly oiled.
- Bake in the preheated oven for 12-15 minutes or until the salmon is cooked through and easily flakes with a fork. Cooking time may vary depending on the thickness of the fillets.
- During the last 5 minutes of baking, brush the reserved glaze over the salmon. This adds an extra layer of flavour and a glossy finish.
- Garnish and Serve:
- Once the salmon is cooked, remove it from the oven.
- Garnish with sesame seeds and chopped green onions for added texture and freshness.
- Serve:
- Serve the Sesame Ginger Glazed Salmon over a bed of steamed rice, quinoa, or sautéed vegetables.
- Drizzle any remaining glaze over the top before serving.

Ingredients

- 4 salmon fillets
- 2 tablespoons soy sauce (or tamari for a gluten-free option)
- 1 tablespoon sesame oil
- 2 tablespoons rice vinegar
- 1 tablespoon fresh ginger, minced
- 2 cloves garlic, minced
- 2 tablespoons honey or maple syrup
- 1 tablespoon sesame seeds (optional, for garnish)
- Green onions, chopped (optional, for garnish)

Beef and Vegetable Kebabs with Cilantro Lime

Directions

- In a bowl, whisk together olive oil, lime juice, chopped cilantro, minced garlic, cumin, paprika, salt, and black pepper.
- Set aside a small portion of the marinade to use for basting during grilling.
- Place the beef cubes in a large bowl or a resealable plastic bag.
- Pour the marinade over the beef, making sure each piece is well coated.
- Seal the bag or cover the bowl and refrigerate for at least 2 hours, or preferably overnight, to allow the flavours to penetrate the meat.
- While the beef is marinating, cut the bell peppers and red onion into chunks suitable for skewering.
- If using wooden skewers, soak them in water for at least 30 minutes to prevent burning during grilling.
- Preheat the grill to medium-high heat.
- Thread the marinated beef, bell peppers, red onion, and cherry tomatoes onto the skewers, alternating between meat and vegetables.
- Place the assembled kebabs on the preheated grill.
- Grill for about 8-10 minutes, turning occasionally, until the beef is cooked to your desired level of doneness and the vegetables are tender and slightly charred.
- During the last few minutes of grilling, baste the kebabs with the reserved marinade to enhance the flavours.
- Once the beef is cooked and the vegetables are tender, remove the kebabs from the grill.
- Serve the kebabs over a bed of cauliflower rice or alongside a fresh salad.

Ingredients

For the Marinade:

- 1/4 cup olive oil
- 3 tablespoons fresh lime juice
- 2 tablespoons fresh cilantro, chopped
- 2 cloves garlic, minced
- 1 teaspoon ground cumin
- 1 teaspoon paprika
- 1 teaspoon salt
- 1/2 teaspoon black pepper

For the Kebabs:

- 1.5 lbs (about 700g) beef sirloin or top sirloin, cut into 1-inch cubes
- 1 red bell pepper, cut into chunks
- 1 yellow bell pepper, cut into chunks
- 1 red onion, cut into chunks
- Cherry tomatoes
- Wooden or metal skewers

Grilled Lamb Chops with Mint Pesto

Directions

- In a bowl, combine olive oil, minced garlic, dried rosemary, salt, and black pepper.
- Rub the lamb chops with the marinade, ensuring they are well-coated.
- Cover the lamb chops and marinate for at least 30 minutes, allowing the flavours to infuse.
- In a food processor, combine mint leaves, parsley, Parmesan cheese, toasted pine nuts, and minced garlic.
- Pulse until the ingredients are finely chopped.
- With the food processor running, gradually add the olive oil in a steady stream until the pesto reaches a smooth consistency.
- Season with salt, black pepper, and lemon juice. Adjust to taste.
- Preheat the grill to medium-high heat.
- Remove the lamb chops from the marinade and let any excess drip off.
- Grill the lamb chops for about 3-4 minutes per side for medium-rare, or adjust the time based on your preferred doneness.
- Arrange the grilled lamb chops on a serving platter.
- Drizzle the mint pesto over the lamb chops or serve it on the side.
- Garnish with additional fresh mint leaves for a vibrant presentation.
- Serve the Grilled Lamb Chops with Mint Pesto alongside your favourite side dishes, such as roasted vegetables or a light salad.
- Enjoy the succulent lamb chops with the refreshing and herby flavour of the mint pesto.

Ingredients

For the Lamb Chops:

- 8 lamb chops
- 2 tablespoons olive oil
- 3 cloves garlic, minced
- 1 teaspoon dried rosemary
- Salt and black pepper to taste

For the Mint Pesto:

- 2 cups fresh mint leaves, packed
- 1/2 cup fresh parsley leaves, packed
- 1/2 cup grated Parmesan cheese
- 1/4 cup pine nuts, toasted
- 2 cloves garlic, minced
- 1/2 cup extra-virgin olive oil
- Salt and black pepper to taste
- Juice of 1 lemon

Pork Carnitas Lettuce Wraps with Pico de Gallo

Directions

- In a large skillet or Dutch oven, heat olive oil over medium-high heat.
- Add the pork chunks and sear on all sides until browned.
- Add diced onion and minced garlic to the skillet. Sauté until the onion is softened.
- Sprinkle cumin, smoked paprika, dried oregano, chilli powder, salt, and black pepper over the pork. Mix well to coat the meat evenly.
- Pour in the chicken broth and lime juice. Bring to a boil.
- Reduce heat to low, cover, and simmer for 2-3 hours or until the pork is tender and easily shredded.
- Shred the pork using two forks and let it simmer uncovered for an additional 15-20 minutes to absorb the flavours.
- In a bowl, combine diced tomatoes, chopped red onion, jalapeño, and cilantro.
- Squeeze lime juice over the mixture and season with salt and pepper. Mix well.
- Refrigerate the Pico de Gallo for at least 30 minutes to allow the flavours to meld.
- Spoon a generous portion of the pork carnitas onto each lettuce leaf.
- Top with a spoonful of Pico de Gallo.
- Optionally, garnish with additional cilantro or a squeeze of lime juice.
- Arrange the Pork Carnitas Lettuce Wraps on a platter and serve immediately.
- Provide extra lime wedges and hot sauce on the side for those who enjoy an extra kick.

Ingredients

For Pork Carnitas:

- 2 lbs pork shoulder, trimmed and cut into chunks
- 1 large onion, diced
- 4 cloves garlic, minced
- 1 teaspoon ground cumin
- 1 teaspoon smoked paprika
- 1 teaspoon dried oregano
- 1 teaspoon chili powder
- 1 teaspoon salt
- 1/2 teaspoon black pepper
- 1 cup chicken broth
- Juice of 2 limes
- 2 tablespoons olive oil

For Pico de Gallo:

- 4 medium tomatoes, diced
- 1/2 red onion, finely chopped
- 1 jalapeño, seeds removed and finely chopped
- 1/4 cup fresh cilantro, chopped
- Juice of 1 lime
- Salt and pepper to taste

For Lettuce Wraps:

- Large lettuce leaves (such as iceberg or butter lettuce)

Lemon Dill Baked Cod

Directions

- Preheat your oven to 400°F (200°C).
- Pat the cod fillets dry with paper towels and place them in a baking dish that has been lightly greased or lined with parchment paper.
- In a small bowl, whisk together the olive oil, fresh lemon juice, lemon zest, minced garlic, chopped dill, salt, and pepper. Ensure the ingredients are well combined.
- Pour the marinade over the cod fillets, making sure each fillet is coated evenly. You can use a brush or spoon to spread the marinade.
- Allow the cod to marinate for about 15-20 minutes. This gives the fish time to absorb the flavours.
- Place the baking dish in the preheated oven and bake for 15-20 minutes, or until the cod is opaque and flakes easily with a fork. The cooking time may vary depending on the thickness of the fillets.
- Once the cod is cooked, remove it from the oven. Garnish with lemon slices and fresh parsley if desired.
- Serve the Lemon Dill Baked Cod hot, accompanied by your favourite side dishes. It pairs well with steamed vegetables, quinoa, or a simple salad.

Ingredients

- 4 cod fillets
- 2 tablespoons olive oil
- 2 tablespoons fresh lemon juice
- 1 teaspoon lemon zest
- 2 cloves garlic, minced
- 1 tablespoon fresh dill, chopped
- Salt and pepper to taste
- Lemon slices for garnish
- Fresh parsley for garnish (optional)

Grilled Steak with Chimichurri Sauce

Directions

- In a medium bowl, combine the chopped parsley, cilantro, minced garlic, red pepper flakes, and dried oregano.
- Stir in the olive oil and red wine vinegar.
- Season with salt and black pepper to taste.
- Mix well and set aside. Allow the flavours to meld while you prepare the steak.
- Pat the steaks dry with paper towels and place them on a plate.
- In a small bowl, mix the olive oil, minced garlic, smoked paprika, and dried oregano.
- Rub the steak with this mixture, ensuring even coverage.
- Season the steaks with salt and black pepper.
- Preheat your grill to medium-high heat.
- Grill the steaks for about 4-6 minutes per side (depending on thickness) for medium-rare, or until your preferred level of doneness is achieved.
- Allow the steaks to rest for a few minutes before slicing.
- Slice the grilled steaks against the grain into thin strips.
- Arrange the sliced steak on a serving platter.
- Drizzle the chimichurri sauce over the steak or serve it on the side.
- Garnish with additional fresh herbs if desired.
- Serve the Grilled Steak with Chimichurri Sauce alongside your favourite side dishes or a fresh salad.
- Enjoy the delicious combination of the perfectly grilled steak and the vibrant flavours of the chimichurri sauce.

Ingredients

For the Steak:

- 2 boneless ribeye steaks (or your preferred cut)
- Salt and black pepper, to taste
- 2 tablespoons olive oil
- 2 cloves garlic, minced
- 1 teaspoon smoked paprika
- 1 teaspoon dried oregano

For the Chimichurri Sauce:

- 1 cup fresh parsley, finely chopped
- 1/4 cup fresh cilantro, finely chopped
- 3 cloves garlic, minced
- 1/2 teaspoon red pepper flakes (adjust to taste)
- 1 teaspoon dried oregano
- 1/2 cup extra-virgin olive oil
- 3 tablespoons red wine vinegar
- Salt and black pepper, to taste

Spaghetti Squash with Bolognese Sauce

Directions

For the Spaghetti Squash:

- Preheat your oven to 400°F (200°C).
- Cut the spaghetti squash in half lengthwise and scoop out the seeds.
- Drizzle the cut sides of the squash with olive oil and season with salt and pepper.
- Place the squash, cut side down, on a baking sheet.
- Bake in the preheated oven for 40-50 minutes or until the squash is tender and easily pierced with a fork.
- Let it cool for a few minutes, then use a fork to scrape the flesh into strands. Set aside.

For the Bolognese Sauce:

- In a large skillet or saucepan, heat olive oil over medium heat.
- Add the chopped onion, carrots, and celery. Cook until the vegetables are softened, about 5-7 minutes.
- Add the minced garlic and cook for an additional 1-2 minutes until fragrant.
- Increase the heat to medium-high and add the ground beef. Cook until browned, breaking it up with a spoon as it cooks.
- Pour in the red wine (if using) and cook for 2-3 minutes, allowing it to reduce slightly.
- Stir in the tomato paste, crushed tomatoes, beef or vegetable broth, oregano, basil, thyme, salt, and pepper. Mix well.
- Bring the mixture to a simmer, then reduce the heat to low. Cover and let it simmer for at least 30 minutes to allow the flavours to meld.
- Adjust the seasoning to taste.

Assembly:

- Spoon the Bolognese sauce over the cooked spaghetti squash strands.
- Garnish with chopped fresh parsley and grated Parmesan cheese if desired.
- Serve hot and enjoy your Primal Gourmet Spaghetti Squash with Bolognese Sauce!

Ingredients

For the Spaghetti Squash:

- 1 large spaghetti squash
- Olive oil
- Salt and pepper to taste

For the Bolognese Sauce:

- 1 pound ground beef (or a mix of beef and pork)
- 1 onion, finely chopped
- 2 carrots, peeled and diced
- 2 celery stalks, diced
- 3 garlic cloves, minced
- 1 can (28 oz) crushed tomatoes
- 1/2 cup red wine (optional)
- 1 cup beef or vegetable broth
- 2 tablespoons tomato paste
- 1 teaspoon dried oregano
- 1 teaspoon dried basil
- 1/2 teaspoon dried thyme
- Salt and pepper to taste
- 2 tablespoons olive oil
- Fresh parsley, chopped (for garnish)
- Grated Parmesan cheese (optional, for serving)

Herb-Roasted Chicken Thighs with Roasted Vegetables

Directions

- Preheat your oven to 400°F (200°C).
- In a small bowl, mix the dried thyme, rosemary, oregano, garlic powder, salt, and pepper to create the herb seasoning.
- Pat the chicken thighs dry with paper towels. Rub each thigh with olive oil and then generously coat them with the herb seasoning mixture, ensuring an even distribution on both sides.
- In a large mixing bowl, combine the halved baby potatoes, baby carrots, sliced bell peppers, and sliced red onion.
- Drizzle olive oil over the vegetables, add dried thyme, dried rosemary, salt, and pepper. Toss until the vegetables are well-coated.
- Line two baking sheets with parchment paper. Place the seasoned chicken thighs on one baking sheet, skin side up, ensuring they are not crowded.
- Spread the seasoned vegetables on the second baking sheet in a single layer.
- Place both baking sheets in the preheated oven. Roast the chicken thighs for about 35-40 minutes or until the skin is golden and the internal temperature reaches 165°F (74°C).
- Roast the vegetables for about 30-35 minutes or until they are tender and slightly caramelized.
- Once the chicken thighs and vegetables are cooked, remove them from the oven.
- Serve the herb-roasted chicken thighs on a plate alongside the roasted vegetables.
- Garnish with fresh herbs like chopped parsley or thyme for an extra burst of flavour.

Ingredients

For the Herb-Roasted Chicken Thighs:

- 4 bone-in, skin-on chicken thighs
- 2 tablespoons olive oil
- 2 teaspoons dried thyme
- 2 teaspoons dried rosemary
- 1 teaspoon dried oregano
- 1 teaspoon garlic powder
- Salt and pepper to taste

For the Roasted Vegetables:

- 2 cups baby potatoes, halved
- 2 cups baby carrots
- 1 red bell pepper, sliced
- 1 yellow bell pepper, sliced
- 1 red onion, sliced
- 2 tablespoons olive oil
- 1 teaspoon dried thyme
- 1 teaspoon dried rosemary
- Salt and pepper to taste

Grilled Salmon with Cilantro Lime Marinade

Directions

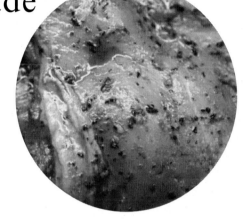

- In a bowl, whisk together chopped cilantro, olive oil, soy sauce, honey (or maple syrup), minced garlic, ground cumin, smoked paprika, lime zest, and lime juice. Season with salt and pepper to taste.
- Place the salmon fillets in a shallow dish or a zip-top plastic bag.
- Pour the cilantro lime marinade over the salmon, making sure each fillet is well coated.
- Seal the dish or bag and refrigerate for at least 30 minutes to allow the flavours to infuse the salmon.
- Preheat your grill to medium-high heat. Make sure the grates are clean and lightly oiled to prevent sticking.
- Remove the salmon from the marinade, allowing any excess to drip off.
- Place the salmon fillets on the preheated grill, skin side down.
- Grill for approximately 4-5 minutes per side, or until the salmon easily flakes with a fork. The internal temperature should reach 145°F (63°C).
- Baste with Marinade (Optional):
- If desired, you can baste the salmon with some of the reserved marinades during grilling for added flavour.
- Serve:
- Carefully remove the salmon from the grill and transfer it to a serving platter.
- Garnish with fresh cilantro and lime wedges.
- Serve the grilled salmon with your favourite sides, such as a refreshing salad, quinoa, or roasted vegetables.

Ingredients

- 4 salmon fillets
- 1/4 cup fresh cilantro, chopped
- 3 tablespoons olive oil
- 2 tablespoons soy sauce (or tamari for a gluten-free option)
- 1 tablespoon honey or maple syrup
- 2 cloves garlic, minced
- 1 teaspoon ground cumin
- 1 teaspoon smoked paprika
- Zest and juice of 1 lime
- Salt and pepper, to taste
- Lime wedges for serving
- Fresh cilantro for garnish

Beef and Vegetable Stir-Fry with Broccoli and Cashews

Directions

- In a bowl, combine the thinly sliced beef with minced garlic, grated ginger, soy sauce, and oyster sauce. Toss well to ensure the beef is evenly coated. Let it marinate for at least 15-30 minutes.

- In a small bowl, mix soy sauce and sesame oil. Set aside.

- Heat vegetable oil in a large wok or skillet over medium-high heat. Add broccoli, bell pepper, and snap peas. Stir-fry for 3-4 minutes until the vegetables are slightly tender but still crisp. Remove the vegetables from the wok and set aside.

- In the same wok, add a bit more oil if needed. Add the marinated beef and stir-fry for 2-3 minutes until it's browned and cooked through. If you want a thicker sauce, you can sprinkle cornstarch over the beef and toss to coat.

- Return the cooked vegetables to the wok with the cooked beef. Add the soy sauce and sesame oil mixture. Toss everything together until well combined. Add the cashews and stir-fry for an additional 1-2 minutes.

- Taste and adjust the seasoning with salt and pepper if necessary. If you like, sprinkle sesame seeds and sliced green onions on top for garnish.

- Serve the Beef and Vegetable Stir-Fry over cooked rice or cauliflower rice.

Ingredients

- 1 lb (450g) beef sirloin or flank steak, thinly sliced
- 2 cups broccoli florets
- 1 bell pepper, thinly sliced (any color)
- 1 cup snap peas, ends trimmed
- 1/2 cup unsalted cashews
- 3 cloves garlic, minced
- 1 tablespoon fresh ginger, grated
- 3 tablespoons soy sauce (or tamari for a gluten-free option)
- 2 tablespoons oyster sauce
- 1 tablespoon sesame oil
- 2 tablespoons vegetable oil (for cooking)
- 1 teaspoon cornstarch (optional, for extra sauce thickness)
- Salt and pepper to taste
- Sesame seeds for garnish (optional)
- Green onions, sliced, for garnish (optional)
- Cooked rice or cauliflower rice for serving

Pork Tenderloin with Apple Cider Glaze

Directions

- Preheat your oven to 375°F (190°C).
- Season the Pork Tenderloin:
- Pat the pork tenderloins dry with paper towels.
- Season the pork with salt and black pepper on all sides.
- In an oven-safe skillet, heat olive oil over medium-high heat.
- Sear the pork tenderloins on all sides until golden brown, about 2-3 minutes per side.
- In a small bowl, whisk together apple cider, maple syrup, Dijon mustard, minced garlic, thyme, salt, and black pepper.
- Pour half of the apple cider glaze over the seared pork tenderloins, ensuring they are well-coated.
- Place the skillet in the preheated oven and roast for about 20-25 minutes or until the internal temperature reaches 145°F (63°C). Baste the pork with the glaze from the skillet halfway through the cooking time.
- Remove the pork from the oven and let it rest for 5-10 minutes before slicing. This allows the juices to redistribute and keeps the meat moist.
- While the pork is resting, place the skillet with the remaining glaze on the stovetop over medium heat. Simmer the glaze until it thickens slightly.
- Slice the pork tenderloin and drizzle the reduced apple cider glaze over the top. Serve with your favourite side dishes like roasted vegetables or mashed sweet potatoes.

Ingredients

For the Pork Tenderloin:

- 2 pork tenderloins (about 1 to 1.5 pounds each)
- Salt and black pepper, to taste
- 2 tablespoons olive oil

For the Apple Cider Glaze:

- 1 cup apple cider
- 1/4 cup maple syrup
- 2 tablespoons Dijon mustard
- 2 cloves garlic, minced
- 1 teaspoon fresh thyme leaves (or 1/2 teaspoon dried thyme)
- Salt and black pepper, to taste

Baked Cod with Tomato and Olive Relish

Directions

- Preheat your oven to 375°F (190°C).
- Place the cod fillets on a baking sheet lined with parchment paper.
- In a small bowl, mix olive oil, dried oregano, garlic powder, salt, and pepper.
- Brush the cod fillets with the olive oil mixture, ensuring they are evenly coated.
- Bake the cod in the preheated oven for 15-20 minutes or until the fish is opaque and easily flakes with a fork.
- In a medium bowl, combine halved cherry tomatoes, chopped Kalamata olives, finely chopped red onion, and fresh parsley.
- In a small bowl, whisk together extra-virgin olive oil, red wine vinegar, salt, and pepper.
- Pour the olive oil mixture over the tomato and olive mixture and toss gently to combine.
- Once the cod is baked, remove it from the oven and transfer the fillets to serving plates.
- Spoon the tomato and olive relish over the top of each cod fillet.
- Garnish with additional fresh parsley and serve with lemon wedges on the side.

Ingredients

For the Baked Cod:

- 4 cod fillets (about 6 ounces each)
- 2 tablespoons olive oil
- 1 teaspoon dried oregano
- 1 teaspoon garlic powder
- Salt and pepper to taste
- Lemon wedges for serving

For the Tomato and Olive Relish:

- 1 cup cherry tomatoes, halved
- 1/2 cup Kalamata olives, pitted and chopped
- 1/4 cup red onion, finely chopped
- 2 tablespoons fresh parsley, chopped
- 2 tablespoons extra-virgin olive oil
- 1 tablespoon red wine vinegar
- Salt and pepper to taste

Lamb and Lentil Stew

Directions

- In a large bowl, season the lamb pieces with salt, pepper, cumin, coriander, and paprika. Toss to coat the meat evenly.
- Heat olive oil in a large, heavy-bottomed pot over medium-high heat.
- Add the seasoned lamb pieces and brown them on all sides. This step adds flavour to the stew.
- Add chopped onions and minced garlic to the pot. Sauté until the onions are translucent and aromatic.
- Stir in diced carrots and celery, cooking for an additional 3-5 minutes until the vegetables begin to soften.
- Mix in the diced tomatoes and tomato paste. Cook for 2-3 minutes to allow the flavours to meld.
- If using wine, pour it into the pot and deglaze the bottom by scraping up any browned bits with a spoon.
- Add the rinsed lentils to the pot.
- Pour in the beef or vegetable broth, ensuring that the ingredients are fully submerged.
- Season the stew with ground cinnamon, and adjust salt and pepper to taste.
- Bring the mixture to a boil, then reduce the heat to low. Cover and let it simmer for about 1.5 to 2 hours, or until the lamb is tender and the lentils are cooked through.
- Taste and adjust the seasoning if necessary.
- Garnish with chopped fresh parsley before serving.

Ingredients

- 1.5 lbs (680g) lamb stew meat, cut into bite-sized pieces
- 1 cup green or brown lentils, rinsed and drained
- 1 large onion, finely chopped
- 3 cloves garlic, minced
- 2 carrots, peeled and diced
- 2 celery stalks, diced
- 1 cup diced tomatoes (fresh or canned)
- 4 cups beef or vegetable broth
- 1 cup red wine (optional)
- 2 tablespoons tomato paste
- 2 teaspoons ground cumin
- 1 teaspoon ground coriander
- 1 teaspoon paprika
- 1/2 teaspoon ground cinnamon
- Salt and pepper to taste
- 2 tablespoons olive oil
- Fresh parsley, chopped (for garnish)

93

Stuffed Acorn Squash with Quinoa and Cranberries

Directions

- Preheat your oven to 400°F (200°C).
- Cut the acorn squash in half lengthwise and scoop out the seeds.
- Place the squash halves on a baking sheet, and cut side up.
- Drizzle a bit of olive oil over the cut side of each squash half, and season with salt and black pepper.
- Roast the acorn squash in the preheated oven for about 30-40 minutes or until the squash is tender and can be easily pierced with a fork.
- While the squash is roasting, rinse the quinoa under cold water.
- In a medium saucepan, combine the quinoa and vegetable broth or water.
- Bring to a boil, then reduce heat to low, cover, and simmer for 15-20 minutes, or until the quinoa is cooked and the liquid is absorbed.
- In a large skillet, heat a drizzle of olive oil over medium heat.
- Add the chopped red onion and garlic, sautéing until softened.
- Stir in the dried cranberries, chopped nuts, dried thyme, and ground cinnamon. Cook for an additional 2-3 minutes.
- Once the quinoa is cooked, add it to the skillet with the sautéed ingredients. Mix well to combine, and season with salt and black pepper to taste.
- Once the acorn squash halves are done roasting, carefully stuff each half with the quinoa and cranberry mixture.
- Place the stuffed acorn squash back in the oven for an additional 10-15 minutes, or until everything is heated through and slightly golden.
- Remove the stuffed acorn squash from the oven and let it cool slightly. Garnish with fresh parsley if desired.
- Serve warm, and enjoy your delicious Stuffed Acorn Squash with Quinoa and Cranberries!

Ingredients

- 2 acorn squash, halved and seeds removed
- 1 cup quinoa, rinsed
- 2 cups vegetable broth or water
- 1/2 cup dried cranberries
- 1/2 cup chopped pecans or walnuts
- 1 small red onion, finely chopped
- 2 cloves garlic, minced
- 1 teaspoon dried thyme
- 1 teaspoon ground cinnamon
- Salt and black pepper to taste
- Olive oil for drizzling
- Fresh parsley for garnish (optional)

94

Seafood Paella with Cauliflower Rice

Directions

For the Cauliflower Rice:

- In a large skillet, heat olive oil over medium heat. Add chopped onions and garlic, sautéing until softened.
- Add the grated cauliflower to the skillet, season with salt and pepper, and stir well to combine.
- Cook for about 5-7 minutes, stirring occasionally, until the cauliflower rice is tender but not mushy. Set aside.

For the Seafood Paella:

- In a large paella pan or skillet, heat olive oil over medium heat. Add sliced bell peppers and sauté until slightly softened.
- Add the mixed seafood to the pan and cook until they start to turn opaque. Season with smoked paprika, saffron threads (if using), salt, and pepper.
- Once the seafood is almost cooked through, add cherry tomatoes, green peas, and cauliflower rice to the pan. Mix well to combine.
- Pour in the vegetable or seafood broth, ensuring that the rice is evenly distributed. Bring the mixture to a simmer, then reduce the heat to low and cover.
- Allow the paella to simmer for 15-20 minutes or until the cauliflower rice has absorbed the liquid and is tender.
- Sprinkle chopped parsley over the paella and gently fluff the cauliflower rice with a fork.
- Taste and adjust the seasoning if needed. Remove from heat.
- Serve the Seafood Paella with Cauliflower Rice, garnished with additional parsley and lemon wedges on the side.

Ingredients

For the Cauliflower Rice:

- 1 large head of cauliflower, grated or processed into rice-like texture
- 2 tablespoons olive oil
- 1 small onion, finely chopped
- 2 cloves garlic, minced
- Salt and pepper to taste

For the Seafood Paella:

- 1 pound mixed seafood (shrimp, mussels, squid, etc.), cleaned and deveined
- 1 cup cherry tomatoes, halved
- 1 red bell pepper, thinly sliced
- 1 yellow bell pepper, thinly sliced
- 1 cup green peas
- 1/2 cup chopped fresh parsley
- 4 cups vegetable or seafood broth
- 2 cups cauliflower rice (prepared from the above ingredients)
- 1 teaspoon smoked paprika
- 1 teaspoon saffron threads (optional, for color and flavor)
- Salt and pepper to taste
- 2 tablespoons olive oil
- Lemon wedges for serving

Shrimp and Broccoli Stir-Fry with Almond Sauce

Directions

- In a bowl, whisk together almond butter, coconut aminos, rice vinegar, sesame oil, honey or maple syrup, and chilli paste. If the sauce is too thick, you can add chicken or vegetable broth to achieve your desired consistency. Set aside.
- In a large skillet or wok, heat 1 tablespoon of coconut or sesame oil over medium-high heat.
- Add the shrimp to the skillet and cook for 2-3 minutes on each side or until they turn pink and opaque. Season with salt and pepper. Once cooked, transfer the shrimp to a plate and set aside.
- In the same skillet, add another tablespoon of oil if needed. Add minced garlic and grated ginger, and sauté for 1-2 minutes until fragrant.
- Add broccoli florets and sliced red bell pepper to the skillet. Stir-fry for 3-4 minutes until the vegetables are tender-crisp.
- Return the cooked shrimp to the skillet with the vegetables, tossing everything together to combine.
- Pour the prepared almond sauce over the shrimp and vegetables. Toss to coat the ingredients evenly with the sauce. Cook for an additional 2-3 minutes, allowing the flavours to meld and the sauce to thicken slightly.
- Once everything is heated through and coated in the almond sauce, remove the skillet from the heat.
- Serve the shrimp and broccoli stir-fry over cauliflower rice, regular rice, or noodles of your choice.
- Garnish with sesame seeds, sliced green onions, or chopped cilantro for added flavour and freshness.

Ingredients

For the Stir-Fry:

- 1 pound large shrimp, peeled and deveined
- 2 cups broccoli florets
- 1 red bell pepper, thinly sliced
- 2 cloves garlic, minced
- 1 tablespoon ginger, grated
- 2 tablespoons coconut oil or sesame oil
- Salt and pepper to taste

For the Almond Sauce:

- 1/4 cup almond butter
- 2 tablespoons coconut aminos (or soy sauce)
- 1 tablespoon rice vinegar
- 1 tablespoon sesame oil
- 1 tablespoon honey or maple syrup
- 1 teaspoon chili paste (optional, for heat)
- 1/4 cup chicken or vegetable broth (optional, for thinning)

96

Herb-crusted Turkey Breast with Cranberry Relish

Directions

- Preheat your oven to 375°F (190°C).
- In a small bowl, combine the dried thyme, rosemary, sage, salt, and black pepper. Mix well to create the herb rub.
- Prepare the Turkey Breast:
- Pat the turkey breast dry with paper towels. Place it on a clean cutting board, skin-side down.
- Brush the turkey breast with olive oil, ensuring it is evenly coated.
- Sprinkle the herb rub over the turkey breast, pressing it into the surface to adhere. Make sure to coat both sides.
- Transfer the turkey breast to a roasting pan, skin-side up.
- Roast the turkey breast in the preheated oven for about 25-30 minutes per pound, or until the internal temperature reaches 165°F (74°C).
- Optionally, baste the turkey breast with pan juices every 20-30 minutes to keep it moist.
- Once cooked, remove the turkey from the oven and let it rest for 10-15 minutes before slicing.

Cranberry Relish:
- Rinse the fresh cranberries and discard any that are damaged.
- In a saucepan, combine the cranberries, orange juice, honey or maple syrup, orange zest, and ground cinnamon.
- Bring the mixture to a simmer over medium heat. Cook for about 10-15 minutes or until the cranberries burst and the sauce thickens slightly.
- Remove the saucepan from heat and let the cranberry relish cool to room temperature.
- Serve the herb-crusted turkey breast slices with a generous dollop of cranberry relish.

Ingredients

- 1 boneless, skin-on turkey breast (about 3-4 pounds)
- 2 tablespoons olive oil
- 2 teaspoons dried thyme
- 2 teaspoons dried rosemary
- 1 teaspoon dried sage
- Salt and black pepper to taste

Cranberry Relish:
- 1 cup fresh cranberries
- 1/2 cup orange juice
- 1/4 cup honey or maple syrup
- 1 teaspoon orange zest
- 1/4 teaspoon ground cinnamon

Sautéed Green Beans

Directions

- Bring a large pot of salted water to a boil.
- Add the trimmed green beans to the boiling water and cook for 2-3 minutes until they are bright green and slightly tender.
- Immediately transfer the green beans to a bowl of ice water to stop the cooking process. This helps them retain their vibrant colour.
- In a large skillet or sauté pan, heat olive oil over medium heat.
- Add minced garlic to the pan and sauté for about 30 seconds until fragrant. Be careful not to let it brown.
- Drain the blanched green beans and pat them dry with a paper towel.
- Add the green beans to the skillet, tossing them in the garlic-infused olive oil.
- Seasoning:
- Drizzle lemon juice over the green beans and sprinkle lemon zest over them for a burst of freshness.
- Season with salt and pepper to taste. If you like a bit of heat, add a pinch of crushed red pepper flakes.
- Sauté the green beans for 3-5 minutes, stirring occasionally. Cook until they are crisp-tender, maintaining a bit of bite.
- Remove the skillet from heat and transfer the sautéed green beans to a serving dish.
- Garnish with chopped fresh parsley for added flavour and a pop of colour.
- Serve the sautéed green beans immediately as a flavorful and vibrant side dish.

Ingredients

- 1 pound fresh green beans, washed and trimmed
- 2 tablespoons olive oil
- 2 cloves garlic, minced
- 1 teaspoon lemon zest
- 2 tablespoons fresh lemon juice
- Salt and pepper to taste
- Crushed red pepper flakes (optional, for added heat)
- Chopped fresh parsley for garnish

Moroccan Spiced Lamb Chops with Cauliflower Couscous

Directions

- In a small bowl, mix the ground cumin, ground coriander, paprika, cinnamon, turmeric, salt, and black pepper. This is your Moroccan spice blend.
- Rub the lamb chops with the spice blend, making sure to coat both sides evenly. Allow the lamb chops to marinate for at least 30 minutes to let the flavours infuse.
- Preheat a grill or grill pan over medium-high heat. Brush the lamb chops with olive oil.
- Grill the lamb chops for about 3-4 minutes per side for medium-rare, or adjust the cooking time to your desired level of doneness.
- While grilling, you can baste the lamb chops with minced garlic and a bit of olive oil for added flavour.
- Once done, remove the lamb chops from the grill and let them rest for a few minutes before serving.
- Garnish with fresh mint leaves before serving.

Cauliflower Couscous:

- In a food processor, pulse the cauliflower until it resembles couscous-sized grains.
- Heat olive oil in a large skillet over medium heat. Add chopped onions and garlic, sautéing until softened.
- Add the cauliflower "couscous" to the skillet and stir to combine.
- Season with ground cumin, ground coriander, salt, and black pepper. Continue to cook for 5-7 minutes, or until the cauliflower is tender but not mushy.
- Taste and adjust seasoning if needed.
- Garnish with fresh parsley before serving.

Ingredients

- 8 lamb chops
- 2 tablespoons olive oil
- 2 teaspoons ground cumin
- 2 teaspoons ground coriander
- 1 teaspoon ground paprika
- 1 teaspoon ground cinnamon
- 1 teaspoon ground turmeric
- Salt and black pepper to taste
- 2 cloves garlic, minced
- Fresh mint leaves for garnish

Cauliflower Couscous:

- 1 head of cauliflower, grated or processed into couscous-sized pieces
- 2 tablespoons olive oil
- 1 small onion, finely chopped
- 2 cloves garlic, minced
- 1 teaspoon ground cumin
- 1 teaspoon ground coriander
- Salt and black pepper to taste
- Fresh parsley, chopped, for garnish

Grilled Halibut with Lemon Herb Sauce

Directions

- Preheat the grill to medium-high heat.
- Pat the halibut fillets dry with paper towels. Brush both sides of each fillet with olive oil and season with salt and pepper.
- Place the halibut fillets on the preheated grill. Grill for about 4-5 minutes per side, or until the fish is opaque and easily flakes with a fork. Cooking time may vary depending on the thickness of the fillets.
- Remove the grilled halibut from the grill and transfer it to a serving platter.
- In a small bowl, whisk together the fresh lemon juice, chopped parsley, chopped dill, chopped chives, and minced garlic.
- Gradually whisk in the extra-virgin olive oil until the sauce is well combined and slightly thickened. Season with salt and pepper to taste.
- Spoon the lemon herb sauce over the grilled halibut fillets just before serving.
- Garnish with additional fresh herbs and lemon wedges.
- Serve the Grilled Halibut with Lemon Herb Sauce with your choice of side dishes, such as roasted vegetables, steamed asparagus, or a light salad.

Ingredients

For the Halibut:

- 4 halibut fillets (about 6 ounces each)
- 2 tablespoons olive oil
- Salt and pepper, to taste
- Lemon wedges, for serving

For the Lemon Herb Sauce:

- 1/4 cup fresh lemon juice
- 2 tablespoons chopped fresh parsley
- 1 tablespoon chopped fresh dill
- 1 tablespoon chopped fresh chives
- 2 cloves garlic, minced
- 1/2 cup extra-virgin olive oil
- Salt and pepper, to taste

Lemon Garlic Roasted Chicken Thighs

Directions

- In a bowl, combine the lemon juice, lemon zest, minced garlic, olive oil, dried thyme, dried rosemary, salt, and black pepper.
- Place the chicken thighs in a large resealable plastic bag or a shallow dish. Pour the marinade over the chicken, ensuring each piece is well coated.
- Seal the bag or cover the dish and let it marinate in the refrigerator for at least 30 minutes, or preferably, overnight for enhanced flavour.
- Preheat your oven to 400°F (200°C).
- Place the marinated chicken thighs on a baking sheet lined with parchment paper or in a roasting pan.
- Roast in the preheated oven for 35-40 minutes or until the chicken reaches an internal temperature of 165°F (74°C) and the skin is golden brown and crispy.
- Once cooked, remove the chicken from the oven and let it rest for a few minutes.
- Garnish with fresh chopped parsley before serving.

Ingredients

- 4 chicken thighs, bone-in, skin-on
- 2 lemons, juiced and zested
- 4 cloves garlic, minced
- 2 tablespoons olive oil
- 1 teaspoon dried thyme
- 1 teaspoon dried rosemary
- Salt and black pepper to taste
- Fresh parsley, chopped (for garnish)

Creamy Mushroom and Spinach Stuffed Chicken Breast

Directions

- Preheat the oven to 375°F (190°C).
- Place each chicken breast between plastic wraps and pound them to an even thickness.
- Season both sides of the chicken breasts with salt and pepper.
- In a large skillet, heat olive oil over medium heat.
- Add chopped mushrooms and sauté until they release their moisture and become golden brown.
- Add minced garlic and chopped spinach, and cook until the spinach wilts.
- Remove the skillet from heat and stir in cream cheese, Parmesan cheese, dried thyme, and dried rosemary. Mix until well combined.
- Lay the pounded chicken breasts on a clean surface.
- Divide the mushroom and spinach mixture evenly among the chicken breasts, placing it in the centre of each.
- Roll up each chicken breast, securing it with toothpicks if necessary.
- In the same skillet over medium-high heat, sear the stuffed chicken breasts until golden brown on all sides. This adds flavour and helps to seal in the juices.
- Transfer the seared chicken breasts to a baking dish.
- Bake in the preheated oven for about 20-25 minutes or until the internal temperature reaches 165°F (74°C).
- While the chicken is baking, make the creamy sauce. In the same skillet, combine chicken broth, heavy cream, and butter. Bring to a simmer and let it cook until the sauce thickens slightly.
- Season the sauce with salt and pepper to taste.
- Once the chicken is cooked through, remove the toothpicks.
- Plate the stuffed chicken breasts and spoon the creamy mushroom and spinach sauce over the top.
- Garnish with chopped fresh parsley.

Ingredients

For the Stuffed Chicken:

- 4 boneless, skinless chicken breasts
- Salt and pepper, to taste
- 1 tablespoon olive oil
- 2 cups fresh spinach, chopped
- 2 cups mushrooms, finely chopped
- 2 cloves garlic, minced
- 1/2 cup cream cheese
- 1/4 cup grated Parmesan cheese
- 1/2 teaspoon dried thyme
- 1/2 teaspoon dried rosemary

For the Sauce:

- 1 cup chicken broth
- 1/2 cup heavy cream
- 2 tablespoons unsalted butter
- Salt and pepper, to taste
- Fresh parsley, chopped (for garnish)

Grilled Swordfish with Mango Salsa

Directions

- In a bowl, whisk together olive oil, fresh lemon juice, minced garlic, dried oregano, salt, and pepper to create the marinade.
- Place the swordfish steaks in a shallow dish and pour the marinade over them.
- Allow the swordfish to marinate for at least 30 minutes, turning the steaks occasionally to ensure even coating.
- In a separate bowl, combine diced mango, chopped red onion, diced red bell pepper, chopped jalapeño, cilantro, lime juice, salt, and pepper.
- Gently toss the ingredients until well combined.
- Refrigerate the salsa to let the flavours meld while you grill the swordfish.
- Preheat the grill to medium-high heat.
- Remove the swordfish steaks from the marinade, allowing excess liquid to drain off.
- Grill the swordfish for about 4-5 minutes per side or until the fish is cooked through and has grill marks.
- Cooking time may vary based on the thickness of the swordfish steaks. The internal temperature should reach 145°F (63°C).
- Place the grilled swordfish steaks on serving plates.
- Spoon the refreshing mango salsa over the top of each swordfish steak.
- Optional: Garnish with additional cilantro and lime wedges for extra freshness and flavour.
- Serve the Grilled Swordfish with Mango Salsa immediately, and enjoy the vibrant flavours!

Ingredients

For the Swordfish:

- 4 swordfish steaks (about 6 ounces each)
- 2 tablespoons olive oil
- 2 tablespoons fresh lemon juice
- 2 cloves garlic, minced
- 1 teaspoon dried oregano
- Salt and pepper to taste

For the Mango Salsa:

- 1 large ripe mango, peeled and diced
- 1/2 red onion, finely chopped
- 1 red bell pepper, diced
- 1 jalapeño, seeded and finely chopped
- 1/4 cup fresh cilantro, chopped
- Juice of 1 lime
- Salt and pepper to taste

Almond Flour Pancakes with Berries

Directions

- In a mixing bowl, combine almond flour, coconut flour, baking powder, and salt. Whisk together to ensure an even distribution of ingredients.
- In another bowl, beat the eggs. Add almond milk, melted coconut oil (or butter), and vanilla extract. Mix until well combined.:
- Pour the wet ingredients into the dry ingredients. Stir until just combined. The batter may be slightly thicker than traditional pancake batter.
- Preheat a griddle or non-stick skillet over medium heat. If needed, lightly grease the surface with additional coconut oil or butter.
- Spoon about 1/4 cup of batter onto the griddle for each pancake. Use the back of the spoon to spread the batter into a round shape.
- Cook the pancakes until bubbles form on the surface, and the edges start to look set. This usually takes 2-3 minutes.
- Carefully flip the pancakes with a spatula and cook the other side for an additional 1-2 minutes or until golden brown.
- Remove the pancakes from the griddle and stack them on a plate. Top with fresh berries and drizzle with maple syrup or honey.
- Serve immediately while the pancakes are warm. Enjoy the delicious, fluffy pancakes with the burst of flavours from the berries.

Ingredients

- 1 cup almond flour
- 2 tablespoons coconut flour
- 1 teaspoon baking powder
- 1/4 teaspoon salt
- 3 large eggs
- 1/2 cup almond milk (or any non-dairy milk)
- 1 tablespoon melted coconut oil or butter
- 1 teaspoon vanilla extract
- Berries (strawberries, blueberries, raspberries) for topping
- Maple syrup or honey for drizzling

Dark Chocolate Avocado Mousse

Directions

- In a small heatproof bowl, melt the dark chocolate chips or chopped dark chocolate using a double boiler or in the microwave. If using a microwave, heat in 20-second intervals, stirring in between until fully melted. Set aside to cool slightly.
- In a food processor or blender, combine the ripe avocados, cocoa powder, melted chocolate, maple syrup or honey, vanilla extract, and a pinch of salt.
- Blend the ingredients until the mixture is smooth and creamy. Scrape down the sides of the blender or food processor as needed to ensure all ingredients are well combined.
- Taste the mousse and adjust the sweetness if necessary by adding more maple syrup or honey. Blend again to incorporate any additional sweetener.
- Transfer the dark chocolate avocado mousse to serving bowls or glasses. Cover and refrigerate for at least 1-2 hours to allow the mousse to firm up and chill.
- Once chilled, you can serve the dark chocolate avocado mousse as is or with optional toppings such as whipped coconut cream, fresh berries, or chopped nuts.
- Serve and enjoy this rich and creamy dark chocolate avocado mousse as a satisfying and healthier dessert option.

Ingredients

- 2 ripe avocados, peeled and pitted
- 1/4 cup unsweetened cocoa powder
- 1/4 cup dark chocolate chips or chopped dark chocolate (at least 70% cocoa)
- 1/4 cup maple syrup or honey (adjust to taste)
- 1 teaspoon vanilla extract
- A pinch of salt
- Optional toppings: whipped coconut cream, berries, or chopped nuts

Berry and Almond Crumble

Directions

- Preheat your oven to 350°F (175°C).
- In a large mixing bowl, combine the mixed berries, granulated sugar, lemon juice, and cornstarch. Toss the berries until they are well coated, and the sugar and cornstarch are evenly distributed. If your berries are very sweet, you can adjust the sugar amount accordingly.
- Transfer the berry mixture to a baking dish, spreading it evenly to cover the bottom.
- In another bowl, combine the almond flour, rolled oats, chopped almonds, coconut sugar or brown sugar, melted coconut oil or butter, vanilla extract, ground cinnamon, and a pinch of salt. Mix until the ingredients are well combined and form a crumbly texture.
- Sprinkle the almond crumble topping evenly over the berry mixture in the baking dish.
- Bake in the preheated oven for 25-30 minutes or until the berry filling is bubbly, and the crumble topping is golden brown.
- Remove from the oven and let it cool for a few minutes before serving.
- Serve the Berry and Almond Crumble warm, optionally with a scoop of vanilla ice cream or a dollop of whipped cream.

Ingredients

For the Berry Filling:

- 4 cups mixed berries (strawberries, blueberries, raspberries, blackberries)
- 1/4 cup granulated sugar (adjust based on sweetness preference)
- 1 tablespoon lemon juice
- 1 tablespoon cornstarch (optional, for thickening)

For the Almond Crumble Topping:

- 1 cup almond flour
- 1/2 cup rolled oats
- 1/4 cup chopped almonds
- 1/4 cup coconut sugar or brown sugar
- 1/4 cup melted coconut oil or butter
- 1 teaspoon vanilla extract
- 1/2 teaspoon ground cinnamon
- Pinch of salt

Espresso Chia Seed Pudding

Directions

- Brew a cup of strong espresso or coffee. Allow it to cool to room temperature.
- In a mixing bowl, combine chia seeds, brewed espresso or coffee, almond milk, maple syrup, vanilla extract, and a pinch of salt.
- Whisk the ingredients thoroughly to ensure the chia seeds are evenly distributed and don't clump together.
- Cover the bowl and refrigerate the mixture for at least 3 hours or overnight. During this time, the chia seeds will absorb the liquid and form a pudding-like consistency.
- After the initial refrigeration period, give the mixture a good stir to break up any clumps of chia seeds and ensure a smooth texture.
- Spoon the espresso chia seed pudding into individual serving glasses or bowls.
- If desired, top the pudding with sliced almonds, a drizzle of maple syrup, or a dollop of coconut whipped cream.
- Serve chilled and enjoy your Espresso Chia Seed Pudding as a delightful breakfast, snack, or dessert.

Ingredients

- 1/4 cup chia seeds
- 1 cup brewed espresso or strong coffee, cooled
- 1 cup unsweetened almond milk (or any other milk of your choice)
- 1-2 tablespoons maple syrup or sweetener of choice (adjust to taste)
- 1/2 teaspoon vanilla extract
- A pinch of salt
- Optional toppings: sliced almonds, a drizzle of maple syrup, or a dollop of coconut whipped cream

Cucumber and Basil Sparkling Water

Directions

- Wash the cucumber thoroughly and slice it thinly. If the cucumber is organic, you can leave the skin on for added flavour.
- Rinse the basil leaves under cold water and pat them dry.
- In a large pitcher, combine the cucumber slices and fresh basil leaves.
- Use a muddler or the back of a spoon to gently press on the cucumber slices and basil leaves. This helps release their flavours.
- Pour the sparkling water into the pitcher with the infused cucumber and basil.
- Stir gently to combine the ingredients. If you prefer a stronger flavour, let the mixture sit in the refrigerator for about 30 minutes to allow the flavours to meld.
- Fill glasses with ice cubes if desired.
- Pour the cucumber and basil-infused sparkling water over the ice.
- Garnish each glass with a slice of lemon for an extra burst of freshness.
- Stir the drink gently before sipping to distribute the flavours evenly.
- Refresh yourself with this crisp and aromatic Cucumber and Basil Sparkling Water.

Ingredients

- 1 medium cucumber, thinly sliced
- 8-10 fresh basil leaves
- 1 liter of sparkling water (plain or flavored, as per preference)
- Ice cubes (optional)
- Lemon slices for garnish (optional)

Coconut Flour Banana Bread

Directions

- Preheat your oven to 350°F (175°C). Grease a standard-sized loaf pan or line it with parchment paper.
- In a large mixing bowl, mash the ripe bananas with a fork or potato masher until smooth.
- Add the eggs, melted coconut oil, honey or maple syrup, and vanilla extract to the mashed bananas. Mix well until the wet ingredients are combined.
- In a separate bowl, whisk together the coconut flour, baking soda, salt, and cinnamon (if using).
- Gradually add the dry ingredients to the wet ingredients, stirring well after each addition. Ensure that there are no lumps in the batter.
- If you're including nuts or chocolate chips, fold them into the batter until evenly distributed.
- Pour the batter into the prepared loaf pan, spreading it evenly.
- Place the loaf pan in the preheated oven and bake for 45-55 minutes or until a toothpick inserted into the centre comes out clean.
- Allow the banana bread to cool in the pan for about 10 minutes. Then, transfer it to a wire rack to cool completely.
- Once cooled, slice the coconut flour banana bread into individual servings. Enjoy it as is or with a spread of butter or nut butter.

Ingredients

- 3 ripe bananas, mashed
- 4 large eggs
- 1/2 cup coconut flour
- 1/4 cup melted coconut oil
- 1/4 cup honey or maple syrup
- 1 teaspoon vanilla extract
- 1/2 teaspoon baking soda
- 1/4 teaspoon salt
- 1 teaspoon ground cinnamon (optional)
- 1/2 cup chopped nuts or chocolate chips (optional)

109

Mixed Nuts and Berries

Directions

- If using raw nuts, you can lightly toast them for added flavour. In a dry skillet over medium heat, toss the nuts until they become fragrant and slightly golden. Be careful not to burn them.
- In a mixing bowl, combine the mixed nuts and fresh berries. You can use a variety of nuts for a diverse flavour and texture profile.
- If you prefer a touch of sweetness, drizzle the honey or maple syrup over the nuts and berries. Toss gently to coat evenly.
- Add a pinch of sea salt to enhance the flavours. Adjust the amount based on your preference for a sweet and salty balance.
- Serve and Enjoy:
- Transfer the mixed nuts and berries to serving bowls or plates. This versatile dish can be enjoyed as a snack, a side dish, or even as a topping for yoghurt or oatmeal.

Ingredients

- 1 cup mixed nuts (almonds, walnuts, cashews, etc.), raw or lightly toasted
- 1 cup fresh berries (blueberries, strawberries, raspberries, etc.)
- 1 tablespoon honey or maple syrup (optional)
- A pinch of sea salt

Deviled Eggs

Directions

- Place the eggs in a single layer in a saucepan and cover them with water.
- Bring the water to a boil, then reduce the heat to a simmer and cook for 10-12 minutes.
- Once cooked, transfer the eggs to an ice water bath to cool quickly.
- Once cooled, peel the eggs and slice them in half lengthwise.
- Carefully remove the egg yolks and place them in a bowl.
- Arrange the egg white halves on a serving platter.
- Mash the egg yolks with a fork until they are well-crumbled.
- Add mayonnaise, Dijon mustard, and apple cider vinegar to the mashed yolks.
- Mix until the filling is smooth and well combined.
- Season with salt and pepper to taste. Adjust the quantities based on your preference.
- Spoon or pipe the yolk mixture back into the egg white halves.
- You can use a piping bag or a simple plastic sandwich bag with the corner snipped off for a neater presentation.
- Sprinkle a pinch of smoked paprika or finely chopped fresh chives on top of each deviled egg for added flavour and a decorative touch.
- Refrigerate the deviled eggs for at least 30 minutes to allow the flavours to meld and the filling to set.
- Serve chilled as a delicious appetizer or snack.

Ingredients

- 6 large eggs
- 2 tablespoons mayonnaise (preferably homemade or a high-quality store-bought version)
- 1 teaspoon Dijon mustard
- 1 teaspoon apple cider vinegar
- Salt and pepper to taste
- Smoked paprika or fresh chives for garnish (optional)

111

Greek Yogurt Parfait with Granola

Directions

- Start by spooning a layer of Greek yoghurt into the bottom of a glass or a bowl. Use about one-third of the yoghurt for the first layer.
- Sprinkle a layer of granola on top of the Greek yoghurt. Ensure an even distribution to add crunch and texture.
- Add a layer of mixed berries over the granola. You can use a combination of strawberries, blueberries, and raspberries. This adds natural sweetness and a burst of fruity flavour.
- Repeat the layering process by adding another layer of Greek yoghurt, followed by granola and mixed berries. Continue until you've used all the ingredients or reached the top of the glass.
- If you prefer a sweeter parfait, drizzle a small amount of honey or maple syrup over the top layer. Adjust the sweetness to your liking.
- Sprinkle chopped nuts (such as almonds or walnuts) over the top for added crunch and a boost of healthy fats. Optionally, sprinkle chia seeds for extra nutrition.
- Serve the Greek Yogurt Parfait immediately and enjoy the delightful combination of creamy yoghurt, crunchy granola, sweet berries, and nutty goodness.

Ingredients

- 1 cup Greek yogurt (unsweetened)
- 1/2 cup granola (homemade or store-bought)
- 1/2 cup mixed berries (strawberries, blueberries, raspberries)
- 1 tablespoon honey or maple syrup (optional, for sweetness)
- 1 tablespoon chopped nuts (such as almonds or walnuts)
- 1 teaspoon chia seeds (optional, for added texture and nutrition)

112

Dark Chocolate Covered Strawberries

Directions

- Wash the strawberries thoroughly and pat them dry with a paper towel. Make sure they are completely dry, as any moisture can cause the chocolate to seize.
- Place the chopped dark chocolate in a heatproof bowl. If desired, add coconut oil to the chocolate to make it smoother when melted.
- Create a double boiler by placing the bowl over a pot of simmering water, making sure the bowl doesn't touch the water. Alternatively, melt the chocolate in the microwave using 30-second intervals, stirring between each interval until fully melted.
- Hold each strawberry by the stem and dip it into the melted chocolate, allowing any excess chocolate to drip off.
- Place the chocolate-covered strawberries on a parchment-lined tray or plate. Ensure they are not touching to prevent sticking.
- Allow the chocolate-covered strawberries to cool and set at room temperature. You can speed up the process by placing the tray in the refrigerator for about 15-20 minutes.
- If desired, melt a small amount of additional dark chocolate and drizzle it over the set of strawberries for a decorative touch.
- Once the chocolate is fully set, serve the dark chocolate-covered strawberries on a platter. They are ready to be enjoyed!

Ingredients

- 1 pound fresh strawberries, washed and dried
- 8 ounces dark chocolate (at least 70% cocoa), chopped
- 1 tablespoon coconut oil (optional, for smoother chocolate)

Zucchini Fritters

Directions

- Place the grated zucchini in a colander over the sink and sprinkle with salt. Toss to combine and let it sit for about 10 minutes. The salt will help draw out excess moisture from the zucchini.
- After 10 minutes, squeeze the grated zucchini with your hands or use a clean kitchen towel to remove as much moisture as possible. This step is crucial to prevent the fritters from becoming soggy.
- In a large mixing bowl, combine the squeezed zucchini, almond flour, Parmesan cheese, chopped parsley, minced garlic, beaten egg, and black pepper. Mix until well combined.
- Heat a skillet over medium heat and add enough olive oil to coat the bottom of the pan.
- Take a small handful of the zucchini mixture and shape it into a patty. Place it in the skillet and flatten it slightly with a spatula. Repeat with the remaining mixture, leaving space between each fritter.
- Cook the fritters for about 3-4 minutes on each side or until golden brown and crispy. Adjust the heat as needed to prevent burning.
- Once cooked, transfer the fritters to a plate lined with paper towels to drain any excess oil.
- Serve the zucchini fritters warm, optionally garnished with additional chopped parsley or a dollop of Greek yoghurt.
- Prepare a simple dipping sauce by mixing Greek yoghurt with a squeeze of lemon juice and a pinch of salt. Serve alongside the fritters for added flavour.

Ingredients

- 2 medium zucchinis, grated
- 1 teaspoon salt
- 1/2 cup almond flour
- 1/4 cup grated Parmesan cheese
- 1/4 cup chopped fresh parsley
- 2 cloves garlic, minced
- 1 large egg, beaten
- 1/4 teaspoon black pepper
- Olive oil for frying

Seaweed Snacks

Directions

- Lay out the nori sheets on a flat surface. If they are too large, you can cut them into smaller squares for bite-sized snacks.
- In a small bowl, whisk together the sesame oil, tamari or coconut aminos, rice vinegar, honey or maple syrup, and sesame seeds. Adjust the sweetness and saltiness according to your taste.
- Using a pastry brush or your fingers, lightly brush each nori sheet with the prepared seasoning mixture. Ensure an even coating on each sheet.
- Sprinkle a pinch of sea salt over the nori sheets for an extra burst of flavour. You can also add more sesame seeds if desired.
- Allow the nori sheets to sit for a few minutes to absorb the flavours. This helps the seasoning adhere to the seaweed.
- Once the nori sheets have absorbed the seasoning, use scissors to cut them into thin strips or bite-sized pieces. This step makes them easy to handle and snack on.
- Your Primal Gourmet Seaweed Snacks are ready to be enjoyed! Arrange them on a plate and serve as a light and flavorful snack.

Ingredients

- 10 sheets of nori seaweed
- 2 tablespoons sesame oil
- 1 tablespoon tamari or coconut aminos (for a soy-free option)
- 1 teaspoon rice vinegar
- 1 teaspoon honey or maple syrup
- 1/2 teaspoon sesame seeds (optional)
- Pinch of sea salt

Avocado and Tomato Slices

Directions

- Wash and dry the avocados and tomatoes.
- Cut the avocados in half, remove the pit, and carefully scoop out the flesh. Slice the avocado into thin, even slices.
- Slice the tomatoes into rounds of similar thickness.
- Alternate the avocado and tomato slices on a serving platter, creating an attractive pattern.
- In a small bowl, whisk together the extra virgin olive oil and balsamic vinegar until well combined. Season with salt and pepper to taste.
- Drizzle the prepared dressing over the avocado and tomato slices. Ensure an even distribution, covering each slice.
- If desired, garnish with fresh basil leaves for an extra burst of flavour and a touch of freshness.
- Serve immediately as a refreshing side dish or a light snack.

Ingredients

- 2 ripe avocados
- 2 large tomatoes
- 1 tablespoon extra virgin olive oil
- 1 tablespoon balsamic vinegar
- Salt and pepper, to taste
- Fresh basil leaves, for garnish (optional)

Carrot Sticks with Guacamole

Directions

- In a medium bowl, combine the mashed avocados, diced red onion, diced tomatoes, minced garlic, and lime juice.
- Mix the ingredients until well combined.
- Season the guacamole with salt and pepper to taste.
- If you like, add chopped fresh cilantro for additional flavour.
- Wash and peel the carrots.
- Cut the carrots into sticks, ensuring they are of a size suitable for dipping.
- Arrange the carrot sticks on a serving platter or plate.
- Place the bowl of freshly made guacamole in the centre of the plate.
- Dip the carrot sticks into the guacamole and enjoy this crunchy and flavorful snack!

Ingredients

For the Guacamole:

- 2 ripe avocados, peeled, pitted, and mashed
- 1 small red onion, finely diced
- 1-2 tomatoes, diced
- 1-2 cloves garlic, minced
- 1 lime, juiced
- Salt and pepper to taste
- Fresh cilantro, chopped (optional)

For the Carrot Sticks:

- Fresh carrots, peeled and cut into sticks

Coconut Yogurt with Berries

Directions

- If using store-bought coconut yoghurt, simply measure out the desired amount. If you prefer homemade coconut yoghurt, you can follow a basic recipe or purchase plain, unsweetened coconut yoghurt.
- Rinse the berries under cold water and pat them dry with a paper towel. If using strawberries, hull and slice them.
- If you prefer a slightly sweeter yoghurt, add honey or maple syrup to the coconut yoghurt. Adjust the sweetness to your liking and mix well.
- In serving bowls or glasses, spoon the desired amount of coconut yoghurt.
- Scatter the mixed berries over the coconut yoghurt. Be creative with the arrangement, or simply mix them in for a burst of colour and flavour.
- Sprinkle shredded coconut over the yoghurt and berries for added texture and a hint of tropical flavour.
- Serve the Coconut Yogurt with Berries immediately. You can enjoy it as a refreshing breakfast, snack, or even a light dessert.

Ingredients

- 1 cup coconut yogurt (store-bought or homemade)
- 1 cup mixed berries (strawberries, blueberries, raspberries)
- 1 tablespoon honey or maple syrup (optional, for sweetness)
- 1/4 cup shredded coconut (optional, for garnish)

Apple Slices with Almond Butter

Directions

- Wash the apples thoroughly.
- Core the apples and cut them into thin slices. You can leave the skin on for added fibre and nutrients.
- Place the almond butter in a small serving bowl.
- Arrange the apple slices around the bowl or on a separate plate.
- Dip the apple slices into the almond butter, ensuring each slice is coated with the creamy goodness.
- If you'd like, please drizzle a bit of honey over the apple slices for sweetness.
- For an extra burst of flavour, sprinkle cinnamon over the apple slices and almond butter. The warmth of cinnamon complements the sweetness of the apples and the nuttiness of the almond butter.
- Enjoy your delicious and nutritious snack! The combination of crisp apple slices and creamy almond butter is satisfying and provides a good balance of fibre, healthy fats, and natural sugars.

Ingredients

- 2 medium-sized apples (choose your favorite variety)
- 1/2 cup almond butter
- 1 tablespoon honey (optional, for drizzling)
- 1 teaspoon cinnamon (optional, for sprinkling)

Kale Chips

Directions

- Preheat your oven to 350°F (175°C).
- Wash the kale thoroughly and pat it dry with a clean kitchen towel. Make sure the leaves are completely dry to achieve crispy chips.
- Strip the kale leaves from the tough stems. You can do this by holding the base of the stem with one hand and pulling the leaves away with the other.
- Tear the kale leaves into bite-sized pieces, keeping in mind that they will shrink a bit during baking.
- Place the torn kale leaves in a large bowl. Drizzle olive oil over the kale and use your hands to massage the oil into the leaves, ensuring each piece is lightly coated. This helps make the kale crispy.
- Sprinkle sea salt over the kale to taste. Optionally, add nutritional yeast for a cheesy flavour. Toss the kale again to evenly distribute the seasoning.
- Line baking sheets with parchment paper. Arrange the kale pieces in a single layer, ensuring they are not crowded to promote even crisping.
- Place the baking sheets in the preheated oven and bake for 10-15 minutes or until the edges of the kale are golden brown and crispy. Keep a close eye on them to prevent burning.
- Remove the kale chips from the oven and let them cool for a few minutes on the baking sheets. They will continue to crisp up as they cool. Once cooled, transfer them to a bowl or airtight container.
- Enjoy your Primal Gourmet Kale Chips as a crunchy and flavorful snack. They are perfect for munching on their own or as a side to other dishes.

Ingredients

- 1 bunch of fresh kale (preferably curly kale)
- 1-2 tablespoons olive oil
- Sea salt, to taste
- Optional: 1-2 teaspoons nutritional yeast for added flavor

120

Protein Balls

Directions

- In a large bowl, combine almond butter, protein powder, honey or maple syrup, shredded coconut, vanilla extract, and a pinch of salt.
- Stir the mixture until well combined. The consistency should be thick and sticky.
- If desired, fold in dark chocolate chips, chopped nuts, or dried fruits to add texture and flavour.
- Place the mixture in the refrigerator for at least 30 minutes. Chilling will make it easier to handle and shape the protein balls.
- Once chilled, take small portions of the mixture and roll them into bite-sized balls. Use your hands to shape them evenly.
- Roll the protein balls in additional shredded coconut, cocoa powder, or crushed nuts for a decorative coating.
- Place the shaped protein balls back in the refrigerator for another 15-30 minutes to firm up.
- Store the protein balls in an airtight container in the refrigerator. They can also be individually wrapped for convenience.

Ingredients

- 1 cup almond butter
- 1/2 cup protein powder (whey, plant-based, or collagen)
- 1/4 cup honey or maple syrup
- 1/2 cup unsweetened shredded coconut
- 1 teaspoon vanilla extract
- Pinch of salt
- Optional: Dark chocolate chips, chopped nuts, or dried fruits for added texture

Almond and Coconut Energy Balls

Directions

- In a food processor, pulse the almonds until they are finely ground. Be careful not to over-process, as you still want a bit of texture.
- Add the pitted dates, almond butter, melted coconut oil, vanilla extract, and a pinch of salt to the ground almonds in the food processor.
- Process the mixture until it forms a sticky dough. If the mixture seems too dry, you can add a little more almond butter or a splash of water.
- Add the shredded coconut to the mixture and pulse until well combined. The coconut will add texture and flavour.
- If you're including optional add-ins like chia seeds or cocoa powder, add them to the mixture and pulse until evenly distributed.
- Scoop out spoonfuls of the mixture and roll them between your hands to form compact balls. The size can vary based on your preference.
- Place the energy balls on a tray lined with parchment paper and let them chill in the refrigerator for at least 30 minutes. This helps them firm up.
- Once the energy balls are firm, transfer them to an airtight container. Store them in the refrigerator for a longer shelf life, or you can keep them at room temperature for a day or two.

Ingredients

- 1 cup almonds, raw and unsalted
- 1 cup shredded coconut, unsweetened
- 1/2 cup Medjool dates, pitted
- 2 tablespoons almond butter
- 1 tablespoon coconut oil, melted
- 1 teaspoon vanilla extract
- A pinch of salt

Optional Add-ins:

- Chia seeds, flaxseeds, or hemp seeds
- Cocoa powder for a chocolatey flavor
- Protein powder for added protein
- Dried fruits such as cranberries or apricots

Celery Sticks with Almond Butter

Directions

- Wash the celery stalks thoroughly under running water.
- Trim the ends and cut the celery into manageable sticks, approximately 4-5 inches long.
- Using a butter knife or a small spoon, spread a generous amount of almond butter into the concave side of each celery stick.
- For added texture and flavour, consider sprinkling a pinch of chia seeds on top of the almond butter.
- If you like a touch of sweetness, add sliced strawberries on top or drizzle a bit of honey over the almond butter.
- Arrange the prepared celery sticks on a plate or tray.
- Serve them as a snack or appetizer for a quick and nutritious bite.

Ingredients

- Celery stalks, washed and trimmed
- Almond butter (unsweetened and preferably natural)
- Optional: Chia seeds, sliced strawberries, or a drizzle of honey for garnish

Mixed Nuts and Dried Fruits

Directions

- Preheat your oven to 325°F (160°C).
- In a large mixing bowl, combine the almonds, walnuts, cashews, and pistachios.
- Drizzle the melted coconut oil over the nuts and toss to coat evenly. The coconut oil will add a subtle flavour and help the seasoning stick.
- If you prefer a slightly sweet flavour, add honey to the nut mixture and toss again to coat. Adjust the sweetness according to your taste.
- Sprinkle sea salt over the nuts, ensuring an even distribution. Toss once more to incorporate the salt.
- Spread the coated nuts in a single layer on a baking sheet lined with parchment paper. This ensures even roasting.
- Roast the nuts in the preheated oven for about 15-20 minutes, or until they become fragrant and slightly golden. Be sure to stir the nuts halfway through the roasting time to ensure even cooking.
- Remove the nuts from the oven and let them cool completely. They will continue to crisp up as they cool down.
- Once the nuts are cooled, transfer them to a large bowl. Add the dried cranberries, chopped apricots, sliced figs, and golden raisins. Toss gently to combine.
- Transfer the mixed nuts and dried fruits to an airtight container or portion them into snack-sized bags for easy grab-and-go.

Ingredients

- 1 cup raw almonds
- 1 cup walnuts
- 1/2 cup cashews
- 1/2 cup pistachios (shelled)
- 1/2 cup dried cranberries
- 1/2 cup dried apricots, chopped
- 1/2 cup dried figs, sliced
- 1/2 cup golden raisins
- 1 tablespoon coconut oil, melted
- 1 teaspoon honey (optional)
- 1/2 teaspoon sea salt

Gourmet Energy Bites

Directions

- In a large mixing bowl, combine the rolled oats, shredded coconut, chia seeds, dark chocolate chips, and a pinch of sea salt.
- Add the almond butter, honey or maple syrup, and vanilla extract to the dry ingredients.
- Mix the ingredients thoroughly until well combined. The mixture should have a sticky consistency that holds together when pressed.
- Place the mixture in the refrigerator for about 30 minutes. Chilling will make it easier to shape the energy bites.
- Once chilled, take small portions of the mixture and roll them between your palms to form bite-sized balls. You can make them as large or small as you prefer.
- For an extra touch, you can roll the energy bites in additional shredded coconut, chia seeds, or crushed nuts.
- Place the energy bites on a plate or tray and refrigerate for at least another 30 minutes to set. After that, transfer them to an airtight container and store them in the refrigerator.
- Your Primal Gourmet Energy Bites are ready to be enjoyed! These make for a convenient and energy-boosting snack. Grab one whenever you need a quick pick-me-up during the day.

Ingredients

- 1 cup rolled oats
- 1/2 cup almond butter
- 1/4 cup honey or maple syrup
- 1/2 cup unsweetened shredded coconut
- 1/4 cup chia seeds
- 1/4 cup dark chocolate chips
- 1 teaspoon vanilla extract
- A pinch of sea salt

Mixed Berries with Coconut Whipped Cream

Directions

Coconut Whipped Cream:

1. Place the can of coconut milk in the refrigerator overnight. This allows the coconut cream to separate from the liquid.
2. Carefully open the can without shaking it. Scoop out the thick coconut cream that has risen to the top and place it in a chilled mixing bowl.
3. Using a hand mixer or stand mixer, whip the coconut cream on high speed until it becomes light and fluffy, resembling whipped cream.
4. Add the maple syrup or honey and vanilla extract. Continue whipping until well combined and fluffy. Adjust sweetness to taste.
5. Place the coconut whipped cream in the refrigerator until ready to use.

Mixed Berries:

1. Rinse the mixed berries under cold water and pat them dry with a paper towel.
2. If using strawberries, hull and slice them.
3. In a mixing bowl, gently toss the mixed berries with honey or maple syrup, if using. This step can be adjusted based on the natural sweetness of the berries and personal preference.

Assembly:

1. Divide the mixed berries among serving bowls or glasses.
2. Spoon a generous dollop of coconut whipped cream over the berries.
3. Garnish with fresh mint leaves, if desired.
4. Serve immediately and enjoy your refreshing Mixed Berries with Coconut Whipped Cream!

Ingredients

For Coconut Whipped Cream:

- 1 can (14 ounces) full-fat coconut milk, chilled in the refrigerator overnight
- 1-2 tablespoons maple syrup or honey (adjust to taste)
- 1 teaspoon vanilla extract

For Mixed Berries:

- 2 cups mixed berries (strawberries, blueberries, raspberries, blackberries)
- 1 tablespoon honey or maple syrup (optional, depending on sweetness preference)
- Fresh mint leaves for garnish (optional)

Gourmet Trail Mix

Directions

- Preheat your oven to 325°F (163°C).
- In a large mixing bowl, combine almonds, walnuts, cashews, pumpkin seeds, and sunflower seeds.
- Melt the coconut oil and mix it with honey (if using).
- Drizzle the coconut oil and honey mixture over the nuts and seeds. Toss well to ensure even coating.
- Add the unsweetened coconut flakes to the nut and seed mixture. Gently mix to combine.
- Spread the coated nuts, seeds, and coconut flakes evenly on a baking sheet lined with parchment paper.
- Roast the mixture in the preheated oven for about 15-20 minutes, or until the nuts are golden brown. Stir occasionally to ensure even roasting.
- Allow the roasted mixture to cool completely on the baking sheet. This helps the nuts and seeds achieve a crunchy texture.
- Once cooled, transfer the nut and seed mixture to a large bowl. Add dried cranberries and dark chocolate chunks. Mix well.
- Sprinkle sea salt over the trail mix and give it a final toss. Adjust the salt to your taste.
- Transfer the Primal Gourmet Trail Mix to an airtight container to maintain freshness.
- Enjoy this gourmet trail mix as a satisfying snack or take it on the go for a quick and energy-boosting treat.

Ingredients

- 1 cup raw almonds
- 1 cup walnuts
- 1 cup cashews
- 1/2 cup pumpkin seeds
- 1/2 cup sunflower seeds
- 1/2 cup unsweetened coconut flakes
- 1/2 cup dried cranberries (unsweetened, if available)
- 1/2 cup dark chocolate chunks (70% cocoa or higher)
- 1 teaspoon coconut oil
- 1 teaspoon honey (optional)
- 1/2 teaspoon sea salt

Veggie Chips with Guacamole

Directions

- Preheat your oven to 400°F (200°C).
- Using a mandolin or a sharp knife, thinly slice the sweet potatoes and zucchini into rounds.
- In a large bowl, toss the sweet potato and zucchini slices with olive oil, sea salt, black pepper, and smoked paprika (if using).
- Arrange the slices in a single layer on baking sheets lined with parchment paper.
- Bake in the preheated oven for 15-20 minutes or until the edges are golden brown and crispy.
- Remove from the oven and let the chips cool on the baking sheets for a few minutes.

Guacamole:
- Cut the avocados in half, remove the pits, and scoop the flesh into a bowl.
- Mash the avocado with a fork or potato masher until smooth but still a bit chunky.
- Add the diced red onion, tomatoes, jalapeño (if using), and chopped cilantro to the mashed avocados.
- Squeeze the lime juice over the mixture and stir until well combined.
- Season with salt and pepper to taste, adjusting the lime and salt as needed.
- Cover the guacamole with plastic wrap, pressing it directly onto the surface to minimize browning.
- Refrigerate for at least 30 minutes to allow the flavours to meld.
- Serve the Veggie Chips alongside the fresh and flavorful Guacamole for a delicious and nutritious snack or appetizer. Enjoy!

Ingredients

- 2 large sweet potatoes, washed and peeled
- 2 zucchinis, washed
- 2 tablespoons olive oil
- 1 teaspoon sea salt
- 1/2 teaspoon black pepper
- 1/2 teaspoon smoked paprika (optional)

Guacamole:
- 3 ripe avocados
- 1 small red onion, finely diced
- 1-2 tomatoes, diced
- 1 jalapeño, seeded and minced (optional for heat)
- 1/4 cup fresh cilantro, chopped
- Juice of 1 lime
- Salt and pepper to taste

128

Raspberry Coconut Chia Popsicles

Directions

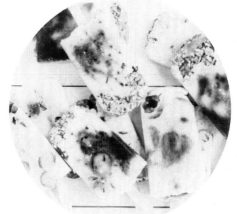

- If using fresh raspberries, rinse them under cold water. If using frozen raspberries, let them thaw slightly.
- In a blender or food processor, puree the raspberries until smooth.
- If you prefer a smoother texture, you can strain the raspberry puree to remove seeds, but this step is optional.
- In a mixing bowl, combine the raspberry puree, coconut milk, chia seeds, honey or maple syrup, and vanilla extract.
- Stir well to ensure that the chia seeds are evenly distributed.
- Allow the mixture to sit for 10-15 minutes to allow the chia seeds to absorb the liquid. Stir the mixture occasionally during this time.
- After the chia seeds have absorbed the liquid and the mixture has thickened slightly, pour it into popsicle moulds.
- If your popsicle moulds have sticks with attached lids, insert them into the moulds. If not, freeze the mixture for about 1-2 hours until it's partially set, then insert popsicle sticks.
- Place the popsicle moulds in the freezer and let them freeze completely, usually for at least 4-6 hours or overnight.
- Once the Raspberry Coconut Chia Popsicles are fully frozen, run the moulds under warm water for a few seconds to help release the popsicles.
- Gently pull the popsicles out of the moulds and serve immediately.

Ingredients

- 1 cup fresh or frozen raspberries
- 1 can (13.5 oz) full-fat coconut milk
- 2 tablespoons chia seeds
- 2-3 tablespoons honey or maple syrup (adjust to taste)
- 1 teaspoon vanilla extract

Cucumber Slices with Hummus

Directions

- Wash the cucumber thoroughly under running water.
- Cut off both ends of the cucumber.
- Optionally, you can peel the cucumber if you prefer, or leave the skin on for added texture and nutrients.
- Slice the cucumber into thin rounds. You can also cut the cucumber into half-moons if you prefer a different shape.
- If using store-bought hummus, transfer it to a serving bowl.
- If making homemade hummus, blend or process chickpeas, tahini, garlic, lemon juice, olive oil, and salt until smooth. Adjust the consistency by adding water if needed.
- Arrange the cucumber slices on a serving platter or individual plates.
- Using a spoon or a small spatula, dollop a small amount of hummus onto each cucumber slice.
- Sprinkle chopped fresh parsley over the hummus for a burst of colour and freshness.
- Drizzle a bit of olive oil over the top for added richness.
- Optionally, sprinkle a pinch of paprika for a hint of smokiness.
- Serve the cucumber slices with hummus immediately as a refreshing and healthy snack or appetizer.

Ingredients

- large cucumber
- 1 cup hummus (store-bought or homemade)
- Fresh parsley, chopped, for garnish (optional)
- Olive oil, for drizzling (optional)
- Paprika, for sprinkling (optional)

130

Guacamole with Jicama Chips

Directions

- Cut the avocados in half, remove the pits, and scoop the flesh into a bowl.
- Mash the avocados using a fork or potato masher until your desired consistency is reached.
- Add the diced red onion, tomatoes, minced garlic, and chopped cilantro to the mashed avocados.
- Squeeze the juice of one lime over the mixture. Adjust the lime juice, salt, and pepper to taste.
- Mix everything until well combined.

Jicama Chips:

- Peel the jicama and slice it into thin, chip-sized pieces.
- In a bowl, toss the jicama slices with lime juice to add flavour and prevent browning.
- Arrange the jicama slices on a serving platter.
- If desired, sprinkle chilli powder and salt over the jicama chips for added flavour.
- Serve the guacamole alongside the jicama chips for a refreshing and crunchy snack.

Ingredients

- 3 ripe avocados
- 1 small red onion, finely diced
- 1-2 tomatoes, diced
- 1-2 cloves garlic, minced
- 1 lime, juiced
- 1/4 cup fresh cilantro, chopped
- Salt and pepper to taste

Jicama Chips:

- 1 medium-sized jicama
- 1 lime, juiced
- Chili powder (optional)
- Salt to taste

131

Greek Yogurt with Walnuts and Honey

Directions

- Measure out 1 cup of Greek yoghurt and place it in a serving bowl.
- Roughly chop 2 tablespoons of walnuts. You can toast them in a dry pan for a few minutes to enhance their flavour if desired.
- Sprinkle the chopped walnuts evenly over the Greek yoghurt.
- Generously drizzle 1-2 tablespoons of honey over the yoghurt and walnuts. Adjust the amount based on your desired level of sweetness.
- If you like, add a few fresh mint leaves for a burst of freshness and colour.
- Give the yoghurt, walnuts, and honey a gentle stir to combine the flavours. Serve immediately and enjoy this delightful and nutritious snack or breakfast.

Ingredients

- 1 cup Greek yogurt
- 2 tablespoons chopped walnuts
- 1-2 tablespoons honey (adjust to taste)
- Fresh mint leaves for garnish (optional)

Conclusion

As we end the pages of *"Primal Gourmet Diet Cookbook,"* I hope you've gone on a culinary adventure that not only delights your taste senses but also feeds your body and spirit. The recipes in these chapters capture the core of the Primal Gourmet philosophy: using whole, nutrient-dense foods to make tasty and fulfilling meals.

Cooking is more than just a daily task; it's an expression of creativity, a celebration of tastes, and a dedication to your health. By using the Primal Gourmet method, you've discovered the delight of making meals that are both tasty and nutritious, demonstrating that healthy eating does not have to sacrifice taste.

Remember, this is more than simply a cookbook; it's a guide to a way of life that appreciates the relationship between the food we eat and the energy we acquire. Whether you're a seasoned chef or a beginner in the kitchen, I encourage you to keep researching, experimenting, and making these recipes your own. Feel free to change the ingredients, add your favourite spices, and make each meal a reflection of your taste.

As you relish the recipes on these pages, I hope you find satisfaction in nourishing your body with the bounty of nature. Share these dishes with your loved ones, gather around the table, and make memories as healthy as the food you've made. Thank you for joining me on this gastronomic voyage — May your kitchen always smell like health, pleasure, and deliciousness.

Happy cooking, and may your Primal Gourmet adventure continue to inspire a lifetime of nutritious and delectable meals.

Vakare Rimkute

Made in United States
North Haven, CT
11 December 2024

62251000R00074